T0303102

Exploration of Selection Bias Issues for the DoD Federal Employees Health Benefits Program Demonstration

Donna O. Farley
Barbara O. Wynn

Prepared for the Office of the Secretary of Defense

National Defense Research Institute | RAND Health

RAND

The research described in this report was sponsored by the Office of the Secretary of Defense (OSD). The research was conducted jointly by RAND Health's Center for Military Health Policy Research and the Forces and Resources Policy Center of the National Defense Research Institute, a federally funded research and development center supported by the OSD, the Joint Staff, the unified commands, and the defense agencies under Contract DASW01-01-C-0004.

Library of Congress Cataloging-in-Publication Data

Farley, Donna.
Exploration of selection bias issues for the DoD Federal Employees Health Benefits Program demonstration / Donna O. Farley, Barbara O. Wynn.
p. cm.
"MR-1482."
Includes bibliographical references and index.
ISBN 0-8330-3121-X
1. Federal Employees Health Benefits Program (U.S.) 2. United States. Dept of Defense—Officials and employees—Health and hygiene. 3. United States. Dept. of Defense—Officials and employees—Insurance requirements. 4. Insurance, Government employees's health—United States. 5. Discrimination—United States. I. Wynn, Barbara O. II. Rand Corporation. III. Title.

RA412.2 .F374 2001
352.6'7—dc21

2002024918

RAND is a nonprofit institution that helps improve policy and decisionmaking through research and analysis. RAND® is a registered trademark. RAND's publications do not necessarily reflect the opinions or policies of its research sponsors.

Published 2002 by RAND
1700 Main Street, P.O. Box 2138, Santa Monica, CA 90407-2138
1200 South Hayes Street, Arlington, VA 22202-5050
201 North Craig Street, Suite 102, Pittsburgh, PA 15213-1516
RAND URL: http://www.rand.org/
To order RAND documents or to obtain additional information, contact Distribution Services: Telephone: (310) 451-7002; Fax: (310) 451-6915; Email: order@rand.org

PREFACE

The purpose of this work was (1) to examine available theoretical and empirical information regarding the issue of selection bias in health plan enrollments and (2) to apply this information to identify the circumstances under which selection might be expected to occur for enrollments in the Federal Employees Health Benefits Program (FEHBP) supplemental health insurance demonstration. This report presents the results of these analyses, including a set of hypotheses regarding risk selection that can be tested in the evaluation of the demonstration. In addition, analytic methods are suggested for use in measuring selection and estimating the extent to which it may occur for enrollments in the FEHBP demonstration.

In recent years, the Congress has asked the Department of Defense (DoD) to conduct a number of demonstrations including the FEHBP demonstration to test ways to enhance medical benefits for Medicare-eligible military retirees. This debate ceased last year when the Congress passed and the president signed legislation establishing what has come to be known as TRICARE for Life (TFL). TFL makes TRICARE a secondary payor to Medicare and entitles Medicare-eligible retirees to these benefits if they have Medicare part B. The present report, therefore, has been overcome by events but still provides very useful information on selection bias that will be important to DoD in examining DoD health care use patterns under TFL and in policy analysis to refine a wide array of medical programs.

This research was conducted for the Department of Defense Office of Health Affairs, within RAND Health's Center on Military Health Policy Research and the Forces and Resources Policy Center of the National Defense Research Institute, a federally funded research and development center sponsored by the Office of the Secretary of Defense, the Joint Staff, the Unified Commands, and the defense agencies.

CONTENTS

APPENDICES

FIGURE AND TABLES

FIGURE

TABLES

SUMMARY

Section 721 of the National Defense Authorization Act for fiscal year 1999 (P.L. 105-261) established a demonstration that allows beneficiaries of the Department of Defense (DoD) health benefits program, who also are Medicare eligible, to enroll in the Federal Employees Health Benefits Program (FEHBP). The three-year demonstration was effective January 1, 2000. The authorizing legislation requires an evaluation of the demonstration that includes consideration of enrollment demand and the demonstration's effects on cost, quality, and access.

The potential DoD costs of an FEHBP option for Medicare-eligible DoD beneficiaries will be determined by the extent to which DoD costs for beneficiaries who enroll in the FEHBP demonstration differ from costs that DoD otherwise would incur for them. One source of cost differences may be risk selection, where beneficiaries who choose the FEHBP option are more or less costly than those who do not enroll.

Recognizing that complex factors influence risk selection, the DoD Office of Health Affairs asked RAND to apply current theory and knowledge to identify how selection bias might occur as Medicare-eligible DoD beneficiaries enrolled in FEHBP plans under this demonstration, and to suggest an analytic approach to estimate the effects of such selection on DoD costs.

DoD beneficiaries who enroll in FEHBP to supplement their Medicare coverage no longer have access to direct-care services by military treatment facilities (MTFs) in the military health system. Therefore, effects of this demonstration on DoD costs will be the net result of several types of changes in costs:

- New costs of the DoD contribution to FEHBP premiums,
- Elimination of MTF costs of care for FEHBP enrollees who had used MTFs, and
- New MTF costs of care for Medicare-eligible beneficiaries who have access to freed up space-available care previously used by FEHBP enrollees.

There likely will be a difference in the size of DoD cost effects for FEHBP premium contributions and for health care services provided by MTFs, and the size of that difference will depend on the extent to which FEHBP enrollees had been users of MTF care. Although the direction of some of these effects may be hypothesized based on economic theory, the net cost effects can only be determined empirically in the evaluation of the demonstration.

DoD may experience other cost effects due to risk selection, where beneficiaries who choose the FEHBP option are more or less healthy (and therefore less or more costly) than the average Medicare-eligible DoD beneficiary. Risk selection can affect two aspects of DoD costs: (1) the actual costs of care for FEHBP enrollees compared to the expected costs that were the basis for the DoD premium contribution, and (2) differences in the costs of care for Medicare-eligible beneficiaries using MTF direct-care services before and after the FEHBP option was introduced. At the start of the demonstration, adverse selection into FEHBP could reduce DoD costs to the extent that more costly beneficiaries discontinued use of MTF direct-care services and shifted to use of services paid for by Medicare plus the FEHBP supplement. In the long run, however, DoD's FEHBP premium contribution will be determined by the health care costs for DoD enrollees and, therefore, would increase as a result of adverse selection. MTF costs of care could decrease more than expected if FEHBP enrollees were sicker than those who remained in the military health system.

PROVISIONS OF THE DoD FEHBP DEMONSTRATION

Medicare pays for about 55 percent of the health care costs for its beneficiaries. To insure against costs not covered by Medicare, many beneficiaries purchase private supplemental insurance, and many enroll in Medicare+Choice plans offering such benefits.

The DoD FEHBP demonstration is one of several options being tested to offer Medicare-eligible DoD beneficiaries expanded choices for supplemental health benefits coverage. The demonstration is being conducted in ten geographic areas. The FEHBP is operated by the federal Office of Personnel Management (OPM). For this demonstration, the OPM manages the plan enrollments for Medicare-eligible DoD beneficiaries as an integral component of the overall FEHBP program. The director of OPM determines subscription charges for self-only and family coverage for plan enrollees, and the DoD is responsible for the government contribution for FEHBP plan enrollees under the demonstration. Beneficiaries eligible for the FEHBP supplemental coverage option include Medicare-eligible DoD beneficiaries who are age 65 or older or who are under age 65 and Medicare-entitled based on disability or end-stage renal disease. Enrollees in the FEHBP program may NOT receive care or pharmacy services from a DoD MTF or enroll in a TRICARE plan.

HEALTH PLAN OPTIONS IN THE DEMONSTRATION MARKETS

Several health plan choices are available in the FEHBP demonstration sites, although the choices vary considerably across sites. Medicare-eligible DoD beneficiaries residing in the sites choose coverage from among the available options, including the FEHBP option. Information on the specific options available in 2000 for each FEHBP demonstration site is provided in the site-specific Appendices C through L. The types of options include the following:

- *Traditional fee-for-service Medicare only*—Benefits are oriented toward acute care services. Participation in Part B (which covers physician and ambulatory services) is voluntary and requires a monthly premium ($45.50 per month in 2000). Gaps in coverage include cost-sharing requirements as well as specific noncovered benefits such as prescription drug and preventive services.
- *DoD benefits*—The only DoD benefits available to Medicare-eligible beneficiaries are space-available care in MTFs (including pharmacy) and additional pharmacy benefits for beneficiaries affected by a Base Realignment and Closure (BRAC) action.
- *Medicare+Choice health plans*—Many areas are served by managed care plans under contract with the Centers for Medicare and Medicaid Services (CMS) to provide coverage for Medicare beneficiaries. These plans cover basic Medicare benefits plus

supplemental benefits such as cost sharing or pharmaceutical coverage. The extent of supplemental coverage varies across markets.

- *Individual Medicare supplemental policies*—Medigap policies supplement traditional Medicare fee-for-service coverage. Most Medicare beneficiaries subscribing to Medigap policies are in traditional Medicare since these policies do not cover Medicare+Choice cost-sharing amounts.
- *FEHBP plans*—Ten nationwide FEHBP fee-for-service plans are available in all demonstration areas, and local health maintenance organization (HMO) or point-of-service (POS) plans that serve individual areas also are available to beneficiaries residing in those areas.
- *TRICARE Senior Prime*—The Medicare-DoD subvention demonstration tested Senior Prime as a military managed care option for Medicare-eligible DoD beneficiaries, where lead agent offices and MTFs served as Medicare+Choice plans. Senior Prime enrollees had priority access to MTF services. The Dover site was in both the subvention and FEHBP demonstrations, and some other sites had overlapping boundaries.

SELECTION BIAS IN INSURANCE

In Section 3, we discuss theoretical aspects of the offering and selection of health insurance options, considering applications of these concepts for the general population, and for Medicare beneficiaries in particular. Both theory and experience have shown that an insurance market can spiral out of equilibrium as a result of adverse selection whenever there are several plan options offering differing benefits and pricing structures (Marquis, 1992; Van de Ven and Van Vliet, 1995; Cutler and Zeckhauser, 1997; Frank, Glazer, and McGuire, 1998). Healthier individuals tend to enroll in leaner, less expensive plans while sicker individuals are willing to pay more for richer benefits. To the extent that richer plans experience adverse selection and higher health care costs, they must increase premiums to cover their costs, which leads to yet more adverse selection and market segmentation. Ultimately, some plans will be driven from the market, leaving high-cost consumers with unacceptable benefits options.

According to insurance theory, good information can help consumers make more effective plan choices and can help insurers manage adverse selection more effectively. Much of the financial uncertainty faced by insurers relates to consumers knowing more about their health status than insurers do. Given this asymmetric information, insurers attempting to price benefits for the expected cost (average) of a group may misjudge the actual health status of the group members, which can contribute to adverse selection. On the consumer side, better information on the costs, benefits, and performance of plans may improve consumers' decisionmaking processes but, ironically, it also may contribute further to adverse selection behavior.

HYPOTHESES FOR SELECTION IN FEHBP ENROLLMENTS

A set of hypotheses was developed regarding expected enrollment and selection behaviors for Medicare-eligible DoD beneficiaries in the FEHBP supplemental insurance option. We hypothesize that beneficiaries residing in demonstration sites that contain MTF catchment areas will be less likely to select the FEHBP option because they would have to forgo utilization of MTF services as FEHBP enrollees. We also hypothesize that beneficiaries currently enrolled in Medicare+Choice plans will be less likely to choose the FEHBP option than those in fee-for-service Medicare because of the transaction costs involved in disenrolling from a health plan to switch to a supplemental insurance policy.

Selection dynamics for the FEHBP option involve two nested stages of selection behavior. The first stage is the decision to switch to FEHBP enrollment from another form of supplemental insurance. The second is choosing a health plan, given the decision to enroll in FEHBP. Selection effects can be expected to occur at each stage, and the net direction of effects must be assessed empirically. Hypotheses developed for the following categories are listed in Section 4:

- *Access to and Use of MTFs*—The preference for military health care on the part of many retired career military personnel and their dependents is well documented, and MTF care is financially attractive because there are no out-of-pocket costs for MTF services. Thus, one may presume that, for beneficiaries in geographic proximity to these facilities, MTF direct-care services would be a strong competitor for FEHBP enrollment.
- *Managed Care*—Enrollees in Medicare+Choice plans typically obtain full benefits from their health plans, including Medicare-covered benefits and supplemental benefits. They will compare their health plan benefits, and the out-of-pocket costs incurred, to those offered in fee-for-service Medicare plus the FEHBP supplemental plan, along with possible transaction costs involved in switching out of their existing enrollments.
- *Fee for Service*—For beneficiaries in fee-for-service Medicare, FEHBP could be quite competitive financially if the federal contribution to premiums yields lower beneficiary premium costs than those for Medigap policies. If FEHBP were a permanent supplemental offering, beneficiaries would assess its value as one offering on a menu of Medigap options. Under demonstration conditions, however, many beneficiaries will be reluctant to take the risk of giving up a desirable insurance package without knowing if the new option will remain available.
- *Good Information*—Information is essential to effective enrollment decisions yet also can influence adverse selection. Factors affecting plan choices and selection effects will include the extent to which beneficiaries are seekers of information and the number and complexity of health plan options from which they must choose.

A SUGGESTED METHODOLOGY TO EVALUATE SELECTION BIAS

Working with the framework of a set of hypotheses, an evaluation can define measures to analyze observed enrollment patterns in the demonstration and to test each hypothesis. In Section 5, we offer a suggested methodology to address two basic policy questions:

1. To what extent does adverse selection occur in Medicare supplemental insurance enrollments for the DoD FEHBP demonstration?

2. If adverse selection is found to occur in FEHBP enrollment choices, how much impact does selection have on DoD health care costs for Medicare-eligible beneficiaries?

The health status or relative risk of each beneficiary is one determinant of his or her health benefit choices and health care costs. The modeling stage of the analysis estimates models of enrollment probabilities in which coefficients on the health status variables represent the magnitude and direction of selection bias. These variables need to be carefully measured so their effects can be interpreted with confidence. The probability of FEHBP enrollment is defined as a function of sets of variables that are likely to be determinants of beneficiaries' enrollment actions, based on the hypotheses:

P(FEHBP) = *f* (demographics, health status/relative risk,
baseline benefit coverage status, access to an MTF,
location characteristics, FEHBP options available,
other coverage options available,
information available on FEHBP and other options,
interactions between health status and plan and market characteristics)

COST EFFECTS OF SELECTION BIAS

Analysis of cost effects of selection should consider (1) DoD costs of MTF direct-care services to the eligible population and (2) costs for the DoD contribution to FEHBP premiums. Costs for any beneficiaries who enroll in FEHBP will shift away from MTF direct-care costs to the FEHBP premium costs. At the same time, costs for MTF care may increase for Medicare-eligible beneficiaries who remain in the system, to the extent that the departure of FEHBP enrollees opens up space-available care for others. Risk selection will affect the FEHBP premium costs if these premiums are experience-rated separately for the Medicare-eligible DoD beneficiaries, subject to a cap on the DoD contribution based on the average costs of civilian enrollees in FEHBP.

To estimate the size of selection bias cost effects, these effects need to be decomposed into two components: (1) the change in DoD costs attributable to beneficiaries switching from their existing benefits to the FEHBP supplemental coverage, and (2) the change in DoD costs attributable to differences in the risk profiles of those who chose FEHBP and those who did not. The following are two basic methods to estimate risk-selection effects on MTF direct-care costs:

- *Comparisons of aggregate costs*—Direct-care costs and beneficiary-months of eligibility are summed within the groups being compared. First, total actual costs and eligibility months are summed, yielding estimates of total costs for all beneficiaries in a group and the average cost per beneficiary-month for the group. Then, total standardized costs and standardized costs per beneficiary-month are summed, where costs are standardized by applying risk scores before aggregating the dollars. The difference between these two sets of costs represents the amount of costs attributable to risk selection.

- *Estimation of multivariate models of determinants of total costs*—Person-level data are used to estimate models in which total direct-care cost is the dependent variable and the risk-score variable is a predictor variable along with variable(s) that define the comparison groups of interest and control for other determinants of costs.

We note that validity of the MTF direct-cost data will determine the quality of the information generated by either of these methods to estimate the cost effects of selection bias. Completion ratios for the Standard Ambulatory Data Record (SADR) outpatient data will have to be used to account for the missing SADR records by adjusting the cost estimates upward. DoD derives completion ratios as the ratio of SADR record counts to Medical Expense and Performance Reporting System (MEPRS) workload counts of outpatient visits for each MTF, outpatient clinic, and month/year.

SECTION 1

INTRODUCTION

Section 721 of the National Defense Authorization Act for fiscal year (FY) 1999 (P.L. 105-261) established a demonstration that allows beneficiaries of the Department of Defense (DoD) health benefits program, who also are Medicare eligible, to enroll in the Federal Employees Health Benefits Program (FEHBP). The three-year demonstration was effective January 1, 2000. The authorizing legislation requires an evaluation of the demonstration that includes consideration of enrollment demand and the demonstration's effects on cost, quality, and access.

POLICY FRAMEWORK

The offering of FEHBP as a supplemental insurance option for Medicare-eligible DoD beneficiaries is one of several options being tested by DoD to provide enhanced health coverage for its Medicare-eligible retirees. Other options considered include TRICARE Senior Prime and TRICARE coverage as supplemental insurance to Medicare, both of which had been tested as demonstration projects. Senior Prime is a Medicare managed care model in which beneficiaries enrolled at one of the military treatment facilities (MTF) and had priority status for obtaining MTF care. This option has been attractive to many beneficiaries because Medicare-eligible beneficiaries normally have access to MTF care only on a space-available basis, which is the lowest priority for all beneficiary groups.

DoD beneficiaries who enroll in FEHBP to supplement their Medicare coverage no longer have access to direct-care services by MTFs in the military health system. Therefore, effects of this demonstration on DoD costs will be the net result of several types of changes in costs:

- New costs of the DoD contribution to FEHBP premiums,
- Elimination of MTF costs of care for FEHBP enrollees who had used MTFs, and
- New MTF costs of care for Medicare-eligible beneficiaries who have access to freed up space-available care previously used by FEHBP enrollees.

There likely will be a difference in the size of DoD cost effects for FEHBP premium contributions and for health care services provided by MTFs, and the size of that difference will depend on the extent to which FEHBP enrollees had been users of MTF care. For example, for FEHBP enrollees who had never used MTF care, the cost effect for DoD would be a growth in costs equal to the sum of the DoD contributions to their FEHBP premiums. At the opposite extreme, for beneficiaries who had been heavy users of MTF care before enrolling in FEHBP, DoD could experience a net savings because its premium contribution would be smaller than the savings gained from eliminating MTF costs for their care. However, some of those savings might be offset by new MTF costs for other Medicare-eligible beneficiaries who enjoyed better access to MTF care with the departure of FEHBP enrollees. Although the direction of some of these effects may be hypothesized based on economic theory, the net cost effects can only be determined empirically in the evaluation of the demonstration.

DoD may experience other cost effects due to risk selection, where beneficiaries who choose the FEHBP option are more or less healthy (and therefore less or more costly) than the average Medicare-eligible DoD beneficiary. Risk selection can affect two aspects of DoD costs: (1) the actual costs of care for FEHBP enrollees compared to the expected costs that were the basis for the DoD premium contribution, and (2) differences in the costs of care for Medicare-eligible beneficiaries using MTF direct-care services before and after the FEHBP option was introduced. At the start of the demonstration, adverse selection into FEHBP could reduce DoD costs to the extent that more costly beneficiaries discontinued use of MTF direct-care services and shifted to use of services paid for by Medicare plus the FEHBP supplement. In the long run, however, DoD's FEHBP premium contribution will be determined by the health care costs for DoD enrollees and, therefore, would increase as a result of adverse selection. MTF costs of care could decrease more than expected if FEHBP enrollees were sicker than those who remained in the military health system.

When estimating the effects of risk selection on DoD costs, an understanding needs to be developed about which factors contribute to any observed favorable or adverse risk selection, followed by assessment of the size of selection effects (if any) on the two aspects of DoD costs identified above. To examine effects on DoD costs for premium contribution, the costs for the DoD FEHBP enrollees should be assessed relative to those for all other FEHBP enrollees because the average costs for the larger group of enrollees serves as a cap for the DoD premium contribution. To examine effects on DoD costs for MTF care, the comparison group is other Medicare-eligible DoD beneficiaries remaining in the military health system. The approach we developed for assessing risk selection effects in the FEHBP demonstration is guided by this policy framework.

SCOPE OF THIS WORK

Recognizing that complex factors influence risk selection, the DoD Office of Health Affairs asked RAND to apply current theory and knowledge to identify how selection bias might occur as Medicare-eligible DoD beneficiaries enrolled in FEHBP plans under this demonstration. Four specific research steps were undertaken to provide information on the issue of selection bias:

- Document the health plan options available to Medicare-eligible DoD beneficiaries residing in the demonstration sites and examine the implications for risk selection,
- Review the theoretical and empirical literature on risk selection to develop a conceptual framework that can be applied to identify selection behaviors that might occur in the DoD FEHBP demonstration,
- Develop a set of testable hypotheses regarding possible risk selection in the DoD FEHBP demonstration, and
- Prepare a methodological approach for evaluating the extent to which risk selection occurred in the DoD FEHBP demonstration and its effects on DoD costs.

This document reports the results of RAND's examination of selection bias issues that may arise in the DoD FEHBP demonstration. These results provide a framework for evaluating the extent to which DoD beneficiaries enrolled in FEHBP differ in their health status and service utilization characteristics compared with (1) civilian enrollees in FEHBP and (2) Medicare-eligible DoD beneficiaries who do not enroll in the demonstration.

As we develop the approach, measures, and analytic methods to address these questions, we consider the availability of DoD data and any data constraints known to us. However, we do not address the more detailed measurement steps that will be necessary for a risk selection analysis, such as coding variables and verifying data availability or designing primary data collection methods. This level of detail is beyond the scope of this study, which was intended to focus on the theoretical considerations of risk selection and their implications for designing a methodology to study selection effects appropriately for the DoD FEHBP demonstration.

PROVISIONS OF THE DoD FEHBP DEMONSTRATION

Summarized here are the basic provisions of the DoD FEHBP demonstration, which provide a factual context for the material presented in this report. The FEHBP is operated by the federal Office of Personnel Management (OPM). For this demonstration, the OPM manages the plan enrollments for Medicare-eligible DoD beneficiaries as an integral component of the overall FEHBP program.

Eligibility and Enrollment Policies

Eligibility for FEHBP is based on eligibility for Medicare and DoD health benefits. Eligible beneficiaries include both those who are age 65 or older and those under age 65 who are entitled to Medicare based on disability or end-stage renal disease. Beneficiaries are not required to be enrolled in Medicare Part B. Eligible beneficiaries may elect a self-only or a family option. The latter option extends coverage to dependents without regard to their eligibility for Medicare. Enrollees may choose and change plans during an annual open enrollment, in the same manner as other FEHBP beneficiaries, and they may disenroll from the demonstration at any time. Beneficiaries who disenroll will not be eligible to reenroll in the demonstration. They are entitled to the same Medigap protections as are available to Medicare beneficiaries who disenroll from a Medicare+Choice plan. Enrollees in the FEHBP program may NOT receive care or pharmacy services from a DoD MTF or enroll in a TRICARE plan. Eligibility to receive services from the Veterans Administration (VA) is not affected.

Financing

The law requires FEHBP to establish separate risk pools for enrollees who are participating in the demonstration for the purpose of establishing premium rates. The director of OPM will determine subscription charges for self-only and family coverage for plan enrollees. The DoD is responsible for the government contribution for FEHBP plan enrollees under the demonstration, except that the DoD contribution may not exceed the amount the government would pay if the electing beneficiary were a civilian federal employee.[1]

Demonstration Sites

The demonstration is being conducted in ten geographic areas selected by DoD and OPM. The authorizing legislation required that the demonstration include

- one area that is a Medicare subvention demonstration site
- one area that includes the catchment area of one or more MTFs
- one area that is not located in an MTF catchment area.

Table 1 displays the demonstration sites. Two sites—Coffee, Georgia, and Adair, Iowa—were not originally designated as demonstration sites. After the initial enrollment period resulted in few enrollments, the enrollment period was extended and these areas were added as demonstration sites. Maps of the demonstration sites are included in Appendices C through L.

ORGANIZATION OF THIS REPORT

In the following sections, we describe the various health plan choices available to Medicare beneficiaries in the demonstration areas (Section 2) and review the literature regarding insurance choices and selection (Section 3). Presented in Section 4 are hypotheses regarding the factors that are likely to influence a beneficiary's enrollment decision. In Section 5, we outline a methodological approach for comparing the characteristics of the three beneficiary populations.

---

1 Under FEHBP, there is a single risk pool for federal workers and retirees. The government's contribution for employees is based on the lower of: (1) 72 percent of the program-wide weighted average premiums for self-only and for self and family enrollments, respectively, and (2) 75 percent of the total premium for the particular plan (OPM, 1999).

Table 1
FEHBP Demonstration Sites

Demonstration Site	Relationship to MTF Catchment Area	Relationship to Subvention Demo
Adair, Iowa (includes all of Iowa outside MTF catchment area and parts of Minnesota, South Dakota, Nebraska, Kansas, and Missouri)	Outside	No
Coffee Georgia (includes parts of Florida, Georgia, and South Carolina outside MTF catchment areas)	Outside	No
Dallas, Texas	Outside	No
Dover Air Force Base, Delaware (includes parts of Delaware and Maryland)	Within	Yes
Fort Knox, Kentucky (includes part of southern Indiana)	Within	No
Greensboro/Winston-Salem/High Point, North Carolina	Outside	No
Humboldt County, California	Outside	No
Naval Hospital, Camp Pendleton, California	Within	Partial overlap
New Orleans, Louisiana	Outside	No
Commonwealth of Puerto Rico	Within and outside	No

SECTION 2

HEALTH PLAN OPTIONS AND GAPS IN THE DEMONSTRATION MARKETS

The Medicare program is administered by the Centers for Medicare and Medicaid Services (CMS, formerly the Health Care Financing Administration (HCFA)). Medicare pays for about 55 percent of the health care costs for its beneficiaries. The main sources of payment for health care costs that are not covered by the Medicare program are beneficiary out-of-pocket payments (19 percent), employer or private Medigap plans (9 percent) and Medicaid (12 percent).[2] Only 13 percent of the total Medicare 65+ population using traditional Medicare fee-for-service rely on Medicare alone for health insurance. About 66 percent have private supplemental insurance purchased through an employer or individually. In contrast, about 68 percent of the elderly enrolled in Medicare+Choice (M+C) plans do not have other coverage, although 25 percent have private supplemental insurance.[3]

MEDICARE BENEFITS

We provide in this section a general description of the health plan choices available to DoD beneficiaries who are eligible for Medicare. In the case of beneficiaries residing in the FEHBP demonstration sites, these choices include traditional fee-for-service Medicare only, Medicare+Choice plans, MTF services, Medigap and employer-sponsored supplemental policies, and FEHBP plans offered in the area. Information on the specific options available in the FEHBP demonstration sites in 2000 is provided in the site-specific Appendices C through L.

The services covered and beneficiary cost-sharing amounts for the traditional Medicare fee-for-service program are listed in Table A.1 in Appendix A. The benefits are oriented toward acute care services. Participation in Part B (which covers physician and ambulatory services) is voluntary and requires a monthly premium ($45.50 per month in 2000).

In addition to its cost sharing requirements, major gaps in the traditional Medicare package include

- outpatient prescription drugs
- routine physicals
- limited coverage for preventive services and mental health services
- long-term care benefits.

---

2 1995 data from the CMS "Current Medicare Beneficiary Survey." Out-of-pocket expenses do not include insurance premiums. HCFA, "Health and Health Care of the Medicare Population," 1995. Available from the CMS web site (www.hcfa.gov).

3 1996 data from the CMS "Current Medicare Beneficiary Survey." HCFA Office of Strategic Planning, "A Profile of Medicare," 1998. Available from the CMS web site (www.hcfa.gov).

- routine dental, vision, or hearing care
- coverage for expenses incurred while outside the United States
- catastrophic limit on out-of-pocket costs.

Outpatient prescription drugs are a major component of beneficiary out-of-pocket expenses. About one-third of beneficiaries have no supplemental insurance to pay for prescription drugs. In 1997, beneficiaries spent an average of $440 out of pocket on prescription drugs and 10 percent of them spent over $1,200 (Kaiser Foundation, 1999).

About 15 percent of Medicare beneficiaries are enrolled in M+C plans, which typically have provided more generous benefits with lower cost sharing requirements than traditional Medicare. An AARP study estimates out-of-pocket costs for managed care enrollees (including premiums) are about 67 percent of the average costs for all non-institutionalized aged beneficiaries (AARP, 1999). However, the level of premiums and generosity of supplemental benefits vary widely. With regard to drug benefits, one out of six Medicare enrollees had no drug coverage in 1999 through their Medicare+Choice plan while one out of four had unlimited coverage (HCFA, 1999a). A Kaiser Family Foundation study found managed care enrollees with high prescription drug usage faced annual drug costs ranging from $1,080–$5,368. The range for beneficiaries with moderate drug needs was $600–$2,700 (Langwell et al., 1999).

For 2000, many Medicare+Choice organizations restructured benefits and increased cost-sharing in response to financial pressures and programmatic challenges. For the first time, all plans have copayments for drugs and the percentage of plans with a dollar cap on drug coverage increased from 75 percent to 86 percent (HCFA, 1999a). In addition, an estimated 327,000 beneficiaries (5 percent of health plan enrollees) were involuntary disenrollees at the end of 1999 because 99 managed care organizations either withdrew entirely from the Medicare program or reduced their service area. Reductions in beneficiary access to any drug coverage took place in Delaware (–42 percent), Iowa (–100 percent), Louisiana (–10 percent), North Carolina (–55 percent), and Nebraska (–100 percent) (HCFA, 1999b). In addition, 975,000 beneficiaries will be affected by Medicare+Choice plan withdrawals or service area reductions in 2001.[4]

DoD HEALTH BENEFITS

When a DoD beneficiary becomes eligible for Medicare at age 65, the beneficiary is no longer eligible for TRICARE. DoD benefits for Medicare-eligible beneficiaries are limited to

- space-available care and prescription drugs from MTFs (including pharmacy)
- pharmacy benefits (including mail order) available only for beneficiaries affected by a Base Realignment and Closure (BRAC) action.

---

[4] FEHBP has experienced many of the same issues as Medicare+Choice plans. For example, premiums increased about 9.5 percent annually in 1999 and 2000. About 20 percent of managed care plans withdrew from FEHBP in 1999 and about 13 percent in 2000 (HCFA, 1999b).

Access to an MTF affects the value of DoD benefits for Medicare-eligible beneficiaries. Access includes (1) geographic proximity to an MTF, (2) range of services provided by the MTF on a space-available basis, and (3) waiting times for appointments. DoD costs may increase if most enrollees in the FEHBP option have limited access to the MTF for medical services.

Dependents of retirees who are otherwise entitled to TRICARE continue to be covered when the member becomes Medicare eligible. As a result, there would be little need for a Medicare-eligible DoD beneficiary to elect the FEHBP family option as a means of obtaining health insurance for a family member.

FEHBP PLANS

There are ten nationwide FEHBP fee-for-service plans available to all beneficiaries residing in the demonstration areas. A summary of the benefits available under the national FEHBP plans is provided in Table A.2 in Appendix A. In addition, local health maintenance organization (HMO) or point-of-service (POS) plans may be available to beneficiaries residing in all or part of a demonstration area.

FEHBP does not require enrollment in Medicare Part B. The standard FEHBP benefits, shown in Table A.2, apply to beneficiaries not enrolled in Part B. For those with Part B coverage, coordination of benefits for Medicare-covered services can be complicated. Medicare is the primary payer unless the beneficiary or spouse is still working and covered by an employer group health plan, including FEHBP. Medicare is secondary when the beneficiary or covered spouse is working and primary when they are retired. When Medicare is primary, the FEHBP plan will typically pay deductible and coinsurance amounts for Medicare-covered services. It may also cover the difference between Medicare's fee schedule amount for Part B services and the physician's charge (which can be up to an additional 15 percent). In addition, the FEHBP plan covers prescription drugs, routine physicals, emergency care outside of the United States, and some preventive services that Medicare does not cover. Beginning in 2001, FEHBP plans were expected to provide mental health and substance abuse parity identical with traditional medical benefits (i.e., the same deductibles, copayments and coinsurance amounts, and day or visit limitations). If the beneficiary is enrolled in a FEHBP HMO and goes outside the plan's network of health care providers, Medicare will pay for Medicare-covered services. The FEHBP HMO copayments for in-network services apply unless the plan waives payment.

INDIVIDUAL MEDICARE SUPPLEMENTAL POLICIES

About 25 percent of Medicare beneficiaries have supplemental Medicare coverage with a privately funded health insurance policy. (An additional 34 percent have employer-funded retiree benefits [Kaiser Foundation, 1999]). Medigap policies are used to supplement traditional Medicare fee-for-service. Most Medicare beneficiaries subscribing to Medigap policies are in traditional Medicare since these policies do not cover Medicare+Choice cost-sharing amounts. Some organizations market Medicare SELECT policies that restrict enrollees to a specific network of hospitals and, in some cases, physicians. The premiums tend to be lower under these policies because the supplemental benefits are payable only when the beneficiary uses network providers. Otherwise, the standard Medigap policy rules apply.

There are ten standard Medigap insurance options that range from covering basic coinsurance amounts to paying for specific services that are not covered by Medicare. The options are summarized in Table 2. Plan A provides certain basic benefits (and must be offered by all Medigap insurers). These benefits are hospital coinsurance and 365 additional hospital days of coverage during the beneficiary's lifetime, Part B coinsurance, and the blood deductible (first three pints). Each of the other nine options provide a different set of additional benefits. Plan J is the most comprehensive set of benefits. When beneficiaries age 65 or older first become entitled to Medicare, they may purchase any Medigap policy that is marketed in the state. However, disabled beneficiaries have limited access to Medicare supplemental policies, with guaranteed issuance being limited to Plan A policies when they first become eligible for Medicare unless state law requires broader access.

Table 2
Supplemental Benefits Covered by Each of the Ten Standardized Medigap Plans

Medigap	Medigap Plan									
Benefits	**A**	**B**	**C**	**D**	**E**	**F***	**G**	**H**	**I**	**J***
Basic benefits	✔	✔	✔	✔	✔	✔	✔	✔	✔	✔
Part A: Inpatient hospital deductible		✔	✔	✔	✔	✔	✔	✔	✔	✔
Part A: Skilled-nursing facility coinsurance			✔	✔	✔	✔	✔	✔	✔	✔
Part B: Deductible			✔			✔				✔
Foreign travel emergency			✔	✔	✔	✔	✔	✔	✔	✔
At-home recovery			✔				✔		✔	✔
Part B: Excess charges						100%	80%		100%	100%
Preventive care					✔					✔
Prescription drugs								✔ Basic coverage	✔ Basic coverage	✔ Extended coverage

SOURCE: HCFA, 2000.

NOTE: Basic benefits include hospital coinsurance and 365 additional hospital days of coverage during the beneficiary's lifetime, Part B coinsurance, and the blood deductible (first three pints).

* Plans F and J also have a high deductible option. This option requires $1,530 out-of-pocket expenses per year before the plans pay anything.

Although Medigap benefits are standardized for each policy option, other policy features vary, which might be important factors for beneficiaries considering the FEHBP option. It is unlikely that a beneficiary would benefit from continuing a Medigap policy while enrolled in FEHBP. However, given the Medicare Current Beneficiary Survey data documenting that 13 percent of beneficiaries have multiple policies (discussed in Section 3), it is likely that some fraction of FEHBP enrollees would keep their other supplemental insurance. Premium rates for most Medigap policies increase as the beneficiary ages, although some are based on age at issue or are community rated. A beneficiary with an issue-age or community-rated policy would be reluctant to give it up for a temporary demonstration program. Underwriting policies and coverage for preexisting conditions are not standard, and another Medigap policy with similar terms might not be available to enrollees leaving the demonstration. The following special rules apply for the FEHBP demonstration:

- A beneficiary who has not been enrolled previously in a Medicare+Choice plan, and who drops a Medigap policy upon enrollment in FEHBP, would be guaranteed reissuance of the same policy if the beneficiary disenrolls from the demonstration within 12 months. A beneficiary who previously has terminated a Medicare+Choice enrollment does not have the same protections.
- At the end of the demonstration, participants have the right to guaranteed issuance of any Medigap policies designated A, B, C, or F that are offered to new enrollees by insurers in the state. While this provides some protection, none of these policy options offer a prescription drug benefit.

The CMS web site (www.medicare.gov) provides information on Medigap and Medicare SELECT policies offered in each site. Premium information is not available on the web site. Information on Medigap policies is maintained at the state level by the State Health Insurance Information Programs (SHIPs), and the states differ in the information made available to consumers. We were able to obtain the names of the companies marketing Medigap policies in each state and, for some states, the specific plans being marketed. However, we could not obtain premium information in most states.[5] Our inability to obtain the premium data also means that the comparative premium information is not routinely available to interested beneficiaries, which will hamper their efforts to make comparisons between the various Medigap policy options and FEHBP.

We were able to obtain detailed policy and premium information for Medigap policies available in North Carolina in 1999. For the age 65 and older population, 29 companies offer Plan A, 27 companies offer Plan F, and only 4 companies offer Plan J. To illustrate the range of premiums within and across the Medigap options, we display in Table 3 the Medigap premiums for ages 65, 70, 75, and 80 for Plans A, F, and J. For comparison, the range of community-rated self-only premiums for the 10 national FEHBP plans is \$65.09–\$286.43 (see Table A.2 for FEHBP premiums for 2000).

---

[5] It may be possible to purchase a data file with premium information from the National Association of Insurance Commissioners (NAIC) that would have aggregate premium information and total insured lives. The file does not have actual monthly premiums.

Table 3
Range of Self-Only Monthly Premiums for North Carolina 1999 Medigap Policies

	Number of Policies	Age 65	Age 70	Age 75	Age 80
Plan A	29				
Attained-age policies	19	$36–61	$43–72	$44–85	$45–101
Issue-age policies	7	40–66	45–69	49–83	51–91
Community-rated policies	1	89	89	89	89
Plan F	27				
Attained-age policies	18	$67–97	$78–112	$92–129	$107–153
Issue-age policies	6	87–118	97–140	105–151	111–168
Community-rated policies	1	103	103	103	103
Plan J	4				
Attained-age policies	2	$176–268	$191–288	$207–288	$219–310
Issue-age policies	1	169	166	174	174
Community-rated policies	1	161	161	161	161

Factors affecting the premium within an option include whether the policy is individual or group, whether it is marketed through agents or direct response, underwriting policies, and treatment of preexisting conditions.[6] The available policies for disabled beneficiaries in North Carolina are Plan A (four policies with premium range of $66–92), Plan B (three policies with premium range of $117–132), and Plan G (one policy with a monthly premium of $66 and a six-months preexisting condition exclusion).

Beneficiaries are more likely to be attracted to FEHBP if the premiums are lower than those they are paying or would need to pay for comparable Medigap benefits. Factors that might influence the decision include the following:

- **Age.** Older beneficiaries covered under an attained-age Medigap policy are more likely to find the FEHBP policy competitive.
- **Current Medigap coverage.** Beneficiaries comparing their Medigap premium to FEHBP premiums are more likely to find savings if they have a high coverage option (e.g., H, I, or J).
- **Drug benefits.** Unlike Medigap and most Medicare+Choice plans, FEHBP plans do not have an annual limit on prescription drug costs.
- **Medicare enrollment status.** Medigap policies supplement traditional Medicare benefits, and beneficiaries pay both the Medicare Part B premium and the Medigap premium. Beneficiaries participating in the FEHBP demonstration are not required to enroll in Medicare Part B.

---

6 *1999 Medicare Supplement Comparison Guide,* Seniors' Health Insurance Information, North Carolina Department of Insurance, Raleigh, North Carolina.

CHOICES AVAILABLE TO BENEFICIARIES

There is considerable variation across the demonstration sites in the choices available to beneficiaries. Medicare+Choice options available in the demonstration sites range from none in Puerto Rico to 14 in the Camp Pendleton demonstration site. We summarize the choices in Table 4 and provide more specific information on the benefits, costs, and quality of each option in the site-specific appendices. In addition to the options listed in Table 4, each beneficiary has the option of original Medicare and the 10 FEHBP plans as well as a range of Medigap policy options. Each plan offered by a Medicare+Choice organization to beneficiaries residing in an area is counted once. (For example, if an M+C organization offers standard and high option plans in the same area, we count this as two options). We include TRICARE Senior Prime in the HMO count where applicable. Within the same demonstration site, the Medicare+Choice plans offered and the cost-sharing requirements for similar benefits may vary by county.

Table 4
Beneficiary Choice in Demonstration Sites

Demonstration Site	Estimated Number of Medicare+Choice Options	FEHBP Site-Specific Options*
Adair, Iowa	IA: 7 HMOs KS: 1–7 HMOs MN: 6–12 HMOs MO: 5–12 HMOs NE: 1 HMO SD: 2 HMOs	IA: 1–4 HMOs KS: 5 HMOs;1 POS MN: 2 POS MO: 0–5 HMOs NE: 0–1 HMOs SD: 0–2 HMOs
Coffee, Georgia	FL: 4–7 HMOs GA: 2 HMOs SC: none	FL: 1–3 HMOs GA: 0–3 HMOs SC: none
Dallas, Texas	10 HMOs	5 HMOs 1 POS
Dover Air Force Base, Delaware	DE: 2–3 HMOs MD: 3 HMOs (excludes Evercare)	DE: 1 HMO MD 2 HMOs; 1 POS
Fort Knox, Kentucky	KY: 4 HMOs IN: 6 HMOs	KY: 3 HMOs; 1 POS IN: 4 HMOs
Greensboro/Winston-Salem/High Point, North Carolina	2 HMOs	2 HMOs 1 POS
Humboldt County, California	4 HMOs	9 HMOs
Naval Hospital, Camp Pendleton, California	14 HMOs	11 HMOs
New Orleans, Louisiana	2–9 HMOs	1 HMO; 2 POS
Commonwealth of Puerto Rico	None	1 POS

* FEHBP options for Adair, Iowa, and Coffee, Georgia based on FEHBP plans offered to civilian employees in demonstration area in 2000. FEHBP options for other demonstration areas based on the number shown on OPM web site (www.opm.gov) with 2000 rates for DoD demonstration beneficiaries.

COMPARISON TOOLS

Beneficiaries have access to tools through CMS (www.medicare.gov) and FEHBP (www.opm.gov) to compare the benefits, cost, and quality of Medicare +Choice and FEHBP plans, respectively. The CMS web site does not provide comparative information on estimated out-of-pocket costs for the various options based on beneficiary health needs. One nonprofit site that does provide this information for Medicare+Choice plans in major population centers is at www.hmosforseniors.com. The FEHBP web site also provides comparative information on estimated out-of-pocket costs by estimated health needs. A beneficiary can use this type of information to determine which plan affords the best protection at the least cost based on estimated health care needs.

SECTION 3

SELECTION ISSUES IN FEHBP BENEFITS FOR MEDICARE-ELIGIBLE DoD BENEFICIARIES

In this section, we discuss theoretical and conceptual aspects of the offering and selection of health insurance options. We consider these concepts as they apply for the general population, and for Medicare beneficiaries in particular. The discussion is organized to yield perspectives on the risk selection implications of offering FEHBP health benefits coverage for DoD beneficiaries who are Medicare eligible.

The issues of costs and risk, which are central to decisions by all participants in a health insurance market, drive the phenomenon of selection bias in enrollments. We begin by defining these two terms and the distinction between them. In considering an insurance contract, consumers, group purchasers, and health plans face uncertainty regarding what their costs would be under that policy. They will know the actual costs only at the end of the policy term, after plan designs are established, enrollment choices are made, and service utilization occurs. Therefore, they must estimate their costs in advance (formally or informally), often with incomplete information. A cost estimate is referred to as the *expected cost*, and the variation in possible costs around the expected cost is the *financial risk*. Statistically, the expected cost is measured as the probability-weighted mean of a set of possible costs, and risk is represented by the standard deviation.

We begin by presenting an overview of basic insurance theory and a theoretical discussion of the motivations and incentives of the three major participants in health insurance markets: the health plans or insurers providing covered services, the major purchasers of the insurance on behalf of a consumer group (i.e., employers or Medicare), and the members of the consumer group (e.g., employee or Medicare beneficiaries). Our focus is on choice behaviors by consumers because risk selection occurs as a result of those choice processes. Then we summarize the empirical information we have gathered from the published literature on the dynamics of plan choice and risk selection, including private-sector insurance markets, FEHBP plans, and Medicare coverage. All of this information is applied to the offering of FEHBP options for Medicare-eligible DoD beneficiaries in Section 4, where we define some hypotheses regarding risk selection that may arise under this supplemental health benefit offering.

HEALTH INSURANCE OVERVIEW

Health insurance was introduced in response to consumers' desire to reduce financial risk. Other things being equal, individuals prefer to pay regular, known premiums to avoid facing unpredictable large costs for health care events. Furthermore, published studies have shown that consumers are willing to pay a premium that is higher than an actuarially fair amount to reduce their financial risk (Marquis and Holmer, 1996; Cutler and Zeckhauser, 1999). The greater an individual's risk aversion, the more value health insurance offers. Yet insurance also creates moral hazard, which is an increased demand for health services due to reduced consumer costs for each unit of health care obtained. Moral hazard creates welfare loss from unnecessary health care costs. Consumer cost sharing has grown in recent years to reduce moral hazard effects and control total health care costs (Manning and Marquis, 1996).

Both theoretical economics and empirical data have shown that an insurance market can spiral out of equilibrium as a result of adverse selection whenever there are several plan options offering different benefits and pricing structures (Marquis, 1992; Van de Ven and Van Vliet, 1995; Cutler and Zeckhauser, 1997; Frank, Glazer, and McGuire, 1998). Healthier individuals tend to enroll in leaner, less expensive plans while sicker individuals are willing to pay more for richer benefits. To the extent that richer plans experience adverse selection and higher health care costs, they must increase premiums to cover their costs, which leads to yet more adverse selection and market segmentation. Ultimately, some plans will be driven from the market, leaving high cost consumers with unacceptable benefits options.

According to insurance theory, good information on the part of both consumers and suppliers can help consumers make more effective plan choices and can help insurers manage adverse selection more effectively. Much of the financial uncertainty faced by insurers is due to the fact that consumers know more about their health status than insurers do. Given this asymmetric information, insurers attempting to price benefits for the expected cost (average) of a group may misjudge the actual health status of the group members. Insurers also lack the information needed to risk adjust premiums for sicker enrollees. On the consumer side, better information on the costs, benefits, and performance of plans may improve consumers' decisionmaking processes, but, ironically, it also may contribute further to adverse selection behavior.

The FEHBP option is being offered to Medicare-eligible DoD beneficiaries as supplemental insurance coverage for benefits not covered by Medicare. It is an alternative to the existing Medicare supplemental (Medigap) policies. The features of health insurance in general also apply to supplemental health insurance. However, consumers' service utilization responses to supplemental insurance can have corollary effects on costs of the primary insurance plan, and such effects have been documented for Medicare. Because most of the Medigap policies cover out-of-pocket costs, moral hazard has led to higher service utilization that has increased costs for Medicare, which still pays a large percentage of provider payments (refer to discussion below).

INSURER RISK IN MEDICARE

In a recent article, Etheredge (1999) reports the results of a dialogue about possible market reactions to the introduction of Medicare drug benefits. Reactions to Medicare provisions in the Balanced Budget Act of 1997 (BBA), including the new Medicare+Choice managed care program highlighted the importance of understanding the perspective of potential contractors. The M+C program has been poorly received by many Medicare health plans. As discussed above, many plans reduced their service areas or withdrew entirely from Medicare contracts, dropping beneficiaries from plan enrollment. This dislocation of the Medicare managed care market is an eloquent example of the importance of understanding the motivation and incentives of all market participants.

The plan representatives and national insurance experts participating in the dialogue raised risk as the pervasive issue for organizations considering participation in a Medicare drug benefit. They identified four aspects of insurer risk, which are relevant for FEHBP options as well:

- Selection risk—uncertainty about the cost impact on the plan when health care needs are unevenly distributed and are predictable to higher-cost patients but not to the plan.
- Cost management risk—uncertainty about how well a plan can control its costs to stay within the capitated payment it receives.
- Government partnership risk—uncertainty that the government will be a good business partner and the contract terms will be predictable.
- Market risk—uncertainty about how the introduction of a prescription drug benefit (or other change) would work to the competitive advantage or disadvantage of insurers or plans.

THEORETICAL MODEL OF HEALTH INSURANCE

When considering issues of DoD beneficiary choices of supplemental health insurance coverage, it is important to take into account the market interactions between the choices consumers are making and the insurance offerings of other important market participants: the health plans being offered and the purchasers offering those plans. Figure 1 summarizes the objectives and relationships of these market participants.

In the long term, all components of the model in Figure 1 will adjust as the market seeks equilibrium among the features of the health benefits offered and the plan choices made by consumers. Yet the preferences of individual consumers—whether employees of a firm, retirees covered by retirement health benefits, a Medicare beneficiary, or a Medicare-eligible DoD beneficiary—ultimately drive the plan options offered by the purchaser (e.g., employer or Medicare). Thus we focus on the details of theory of consumer preferences and choices in the discussion below, while providing similar detail for health plans and purchasers in Appendix B.

Consumers in the workforce make choices at two levels that involve evaluation of the health plan options available to them. First, consumers consider the health benefits offered by potential employers when seeking employment in the labor market. Then, once an individual has become a worker for a firm, or is retired and a Medicare beneficiary, the utility of health benefits plays a role in his or her health plan choice. According to utility theory, a consumer will make a health plan choice that will maximize his or her utility. In the case of insurance choice, the consumer's utility is a function of net income (or wealth) after insurance costs, the generosity of insurance benefits, and health status.

Two important factors in consumer health plan choices are inherent to any insurance market. First, the consumer preferences that guide their choices of health benefits drive many of the performance outcomes of insurance suppliers and group purchasers. These consumer preferences are taken into account by insurers as they design the options they offer, as well as by group purchasers as they select the set of plans they will offer to their employees or beneficiaries. Second, the insurers and purchasers face financial uncertainty with respect to how many people will enroll in each plan, as well as to how costly their health care utilization will be. When insurers and purchasers face high financial risk due to heterogeneity in consumers' health status, or uncertainty in the information available to them, they will structure benefit configurations, premiums, and cost-sharing provisions to reduce that risk.

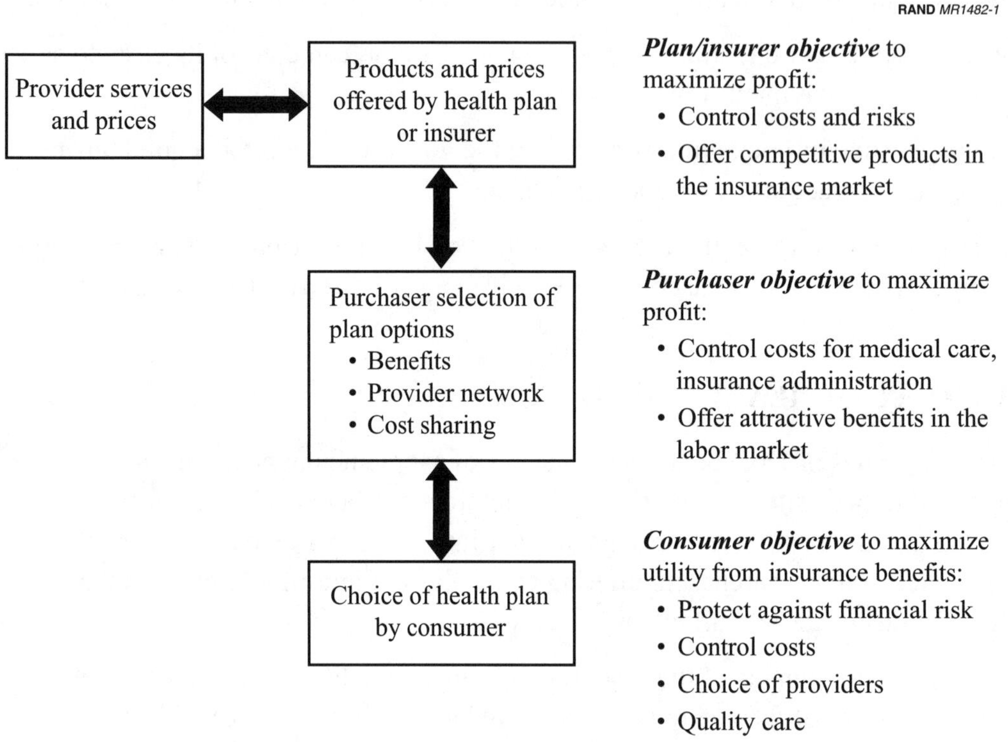

Figure 1—Participants in a Health Insurance Market

FACTORS CONTRIBUTING TO ADVERSE SELECTION

For the FEHBP demonstration, the FEHBP plan options are fixed by the Office of Personnel Management. The same is true for the other plan options available through the Medicare program, including both M+C plans and fee-for-service Medicare with supplemental Medigap insurance. Therefore, the only element of our theoretical model that is subject to change in the demonstration in the shorter term is the amount of information that beneficiaries obtain about their insurance options. A goal of the evaluation should be to observe and document carefully the status of the non-varying factors at each demonstration site so that differences among them can be related to enrollment and selection outcomes for the FEHBP options. The descriptive materials in Appendices C through L about the coverage options available to beneficiaries in the demonstration sites provide information on many of those factors.

Plan Benefits, Costs, and Performance

Empirical research has documented that multiple factors play important roles in health plan choices, including the services covered, premiums and out-of-pocket costs to the consumer, maintaining established relationships with providers, and freedom of provider choice (Mechanic, Ettel, and Davis, 1990; Marquis and Rogowski, 1991; Davis et al., 1995; Scanlon, Chernew, and Lave, 1997, Sainfort and Booske, 1996; Gibbs, Sangl, and Burrus, 1996; Tumlinson et al., 1997). When making health plan choices, consumers seem to give a lower priority to considerations of quality and service than the scope and generosity of coverage, premium costs, or provider choice (Sainfort and Booske, 1996; Castles, Goodwin, and Damberg, 1997; Knutson et al., 1997; Robinson and Brodie, 1997; Tumlinson et al., 1997; Chernew and Scanlon, 1998). However, Sainfort and Booske (1996) found that consumers' use of plan performance information tends to increase as they are exposed to the information and learn how to interpret it.

Adverse selection is an inherent issue for individual choice of health insurance policies, where consumers of differing health status and expected health care costs may sort themselves across plans. In examining effects of adverse selection, however, it is important to distinguish the separate effects of adverse selection and moral hazard, both of which yield higher rates of service use (Van de Ven and Van Vliet, 1995). Three types of losses are induced by adverse selection: efficiency losses from individuals enrolling in the wrong plans for their needs, risk sharing losses as segmentation increases variability of plan premiums, and losses from insurers distorting their policies to improve their mix of insured (Cutler and Zeckhauser, 1997; Frank, Glazer, and McGuire, 1998).

Purchasers can influence the extent to which adverse selection occurs by how they structure their contributions to plan premiums. Field experience and research has shown that equal (fixed) purchaser contributions to all insurance plans can exacerbate market segmentation because consumers face the full amount of incremental cost over the purchaser's contribution. On the other hand, purchasers can contain adverse selection using contributions that are proportional to premiums, under which a higher fraction of employees will choose high-cost, high-benefit options than would be true under a fixed purchaser contribution (Marquis, 1992; Cutler and Reber, 1996; Cutler and Zeckhauser, 1997; Marquis and Buchanan, 1999).

As we discuss below in greater detail, the government contribution to FEHBP premiums is a proportional contribution, where the government pays 75 percent of any plan premium up to a specified "cap," a maximum that is established by legislation. This design is intended to mitigate adverse selection in FEHBP by making the plans with higher premiums relatively less costly for beneficiaries than they would be if the government paid a fixed dollar amount.

Field experience has shown that plan switching stimulated by introduction of fixed purchaser contributions can segment insurance markets and ultimately may lead to exit of the most generous policies from a market. These results occurred in the cases when Harvard University and the University of California changed policies to limit their contributions to the cost of the least expensive plans. Strong price elasticity in consumer demand was observed as employees who experienced premium increases switched to health plans with lower premiums.

(Cutler and Reber, 1996; Buchmueller and Feldstein, 1997). When Harvard took this action, the resulting adverse selection led to the discontinuation of the most generous plan offered.

In addition to proportional purchaser contributions, other methods identified to mitigate adverse selection are risk-adjusted premiums, reinsurance for high-cost cases, offering consumers the choice of a full premium or a deductible with a reduced premium, and use of contracts with a two-year life instead of one year. Analyses suggest that these methods, alone or in combination, can reduce adverse selection due to asymmetric information (Van de Ven and Van Vliet, 1995; Cutler and Zeckhauser, 1997).

Theoretical models of adverse selection assume that consumers have no transaction costs to switch from one benefit plan to another. In actual practice, consumers might face substantial transaction costs in the form of time to collect and evaluate information on their choices, administrative paperwork, and changes in health care providers. Only if the value of switching plans outweighed these transaction costs would consumers make a change, and, therefore, we would expect price elasticity to be lower for consumers with higher transaction costs (Neipp and Zeckhauser, 1985; Van de Ven and Van Vliet, 1995).

How Information Influences Coverage Choices

A growing body of published research reveals the challenges involved in providing effective information to consumers in ways that will help them make well-informed health plan choices. Although there is some empirical evidence that consumers are likely to consider information about plan performance when it is available, the evidence is mixed about how they use it and about its relative importance in their decisionmaking (Scanlon, Chernew, and Lave, 1997). A survey of employees of firms in the Minneapolis Buyers Health Care Action Group found that employees tended to trust information provided by their employers, and they tended to use more than one source of information. This study concluded that use of information is specific to the local situation and cannot be generalized readily (Feldman, Christianson, and Schultz, 2000).

The Consumer Assessment of Health Plans Study (CAHPS®) was initiated in 1995 by the Agency for Health Care Policy and Research (now the Agency for Healthcare Research and Quality, AHRQ) to develop and test survey and reporting tools to help consumers choose plans by giving them information from a survey of plan members (Crofton, Lubalin, and Darby, 1999). Demonstrations and evaluations of CAHPS information have found that when consumers (either privately insured or Medicaid) were exposed to CAHPS reports under the "ideal" conditions of a laboratory setting, they were more likely to choose health plans that performed better according to the reports, but the CAHPS information had much weaker effects on plan choices under field conditions. In a field experiment with the New Jersey Medicaid program, CAHPS information was found to have some effect on choice for a subset of the study sample of new beneficiaries who were identified as proactive decisionmakers. This subgroup chose HMOs with better CAHPS ratings at a slightly higher rate than an equivalent control group, after controlling for other factors that influenced their plan choices, including the popularity of an HMO with a large Medicaid market share that scored poorly on the CAHPS performance measures (Spranca et al., 2000; Kanouse et al., 2000; Farley et al., in press).

Better information on benefits, costs, and plan performance may influence selection bias in plan enrollments, but there is little information in the literature on this matter. One study that examined this issue estimated that imperfect information for Medicare beneficiaries increased the probability of choosing not to purchase supplemental insurance by about 23 percent. This effect was the result of increasing the variance of the distribution of consumers' expected benefits instead of shifting the mean of the distribution (Gertler, Sturm, and Davidson, 1994).

SELECTION ISSUES IN MEDICARE AND FEHBP

A great deal of published research is available regarding the demand for Medicare supplemental insurance coverage and FEHBP benefits, including those for retired and Medicare-eligible federal employees. There is also a useful body of knowledge regarding the impacts of supplemental coverage on subsequent health care utilization, which has spillover effects for Medicare costs.

Supplemental Insurance in the Medicare Program

As reported in Section 2, a majority of Medicare beneficiaries have supplemental insurance, and only 11 percent are covered by fee-for-service Medicare alone. These facts highlight the substantial demand for Medicare supplemental insurance coverage.

Research results vary regarding the factors that contribute to demand for supplemental insurance, which differs somewhat for individually purchased Medigap policies and employer-sponsored retiree health benefits. Wealth has been found to be one of the strongest predictors of having individually purchased Medigap coverage, and job tenure and occupation are important predictors of employer-based supplemental insurance. Supplemental insurance is also present at higher rates for higher educational levels (Taylor, Farley, and Horgan, 1988; Wolfe and Goddeeris, 1991; Ettner, 1997; Lillard, Rogowski, and Kington, 1997). Although health status is a determinant of supplemental insurance coverage, research findings are mixed with respect to the strength and direction of effect. Some studies found evidence of adverse selection (i.e., higher rates of supplemental coverage for beneficiaries with poorer health status), some found no significant effects, and others found that people in poorer health were less likely to purchase Medigap insurance. In addition to replicating findings for financial and demographic determinants of Medigap purchase, one study found that individuals with positive attitudes toward health care and physicians were more likely to purchase supplemental insurance, specifically for drug coverage, and those who reported they take risks were less likely to purchase Part A deductible coverage (Vistnes and Banthin, 1997).

Another important aspect of Medigap insurance is its moral hazard effect of stimulating additional service utilization and escalating health care costs. Cost-sharing benefits provide almost "first dollar" coverage for Medicare beneficiaries. Several studies have found higher utilization and costs for those with either individually purchased Medigap coverage or employer-based coverage, with stronger effects for Part B services (Lillard and Rogowski, 1995; O'Connell, 1996; PPRC, 1996; Christensen and Shinogle, 1997; Khandker and McCormack, 1999). Of interest, these studies generated quite similar estimates of spending effects, despite using different data sources. Christensen and Shinogle estimated that compared to Medicare beneficiaries with no insurance supplement, service use was 28 percent higher for those with individual Medigap policies and 17 percent higher for those with employer-sponsored plans. Only Medicare managed care plans reduced cost sharing without increasing overall use of services. These results compared closely with findings of the Physician Payment Review Commission (1996).

The selection bias issue may be important for prescription drug coverage because the heaviest users of prescription drugs are people with chronic health problems. There is little information in the literature that directly addresses this issue, but given the weak evidence for adverse selection for overall supplemental coverage, whatever contribution that drug coverage may make to overall selection bias may be too small to be visible. To test this issue directly would require modeling demand for individual types of Medigap policies with comparison of results for those that do and do not offer drug benefits. One study of drug coverage effects on use and expenditures in the Medicare population found higher probability of increased use of prescription drugs but no effect on expenditures (Lillard, Rogowski, and Kington, 1999). Drug coverage has been found to stimulate substitution of prescription drugs for cheaper over-the-counter drugs because the prescription drugs costs were lower for the insured consumer (Stuart and Grana, 1995).

Information for Medicare beneficiaries on supplemental policies has been an issue for years, and it was one of the factors that led to the reform of Medigap insurance by the Omnibus Budget Reconciliation Act of 1990. A General Accounting Office (GAO) study found that in 1991 an estimated 13 percent of beneficiaries had multiple supplemental policies through various combinations of employer-sponsored plans, individually purchased policies, or Medicaid coverage (Dowdal et al., 1994). Policymakers have interpreted this finding as a symptom of consumer confusion. Multiple coverage continues today, although the extent of it appears to have abated somewhat. According to an evaluation of the new standardized policies, Medigap reform achieved its objectives of enabling beneficiaries to make more informed choices and correcting marketing abuses, while protecting the integrity of the supplemental insurance market (McCormack et al., 1996). The smaller number of plans offered reportedly has made the decision process more manageable, while still providing beneficiaries sufficient choices.

Experiences in the FEHBP

The FEHBP evolved informally during the early 1960s, ultimately taking the form it has today of a diverse set of health plan offerings where the health plans assume all the financial risk for covered beneficiaries. Both current employees and retirees of the federal government have health insurance coverage under FEHBP, with a choice among this variety of health plans. In contrast to the Medicare program, OPM functions are limited to negotiating contract terms with participating plans, collection and payment of plan premiums, overseeing plan performance, and providing information for beneficiaries. The health plans are responsible for claims processing for health care services provided to their FEHBP enrollees.

Because of the program's long, apparently successful, history, some policy analysts have been advocating use of the FEHBP model for reform of the Medicare program. Ironically, just the reverse argument was made in the early 1990s as the Clinton health reform proposal was being debated, when there were concerns about effects of adverse selection on the stability of the FEHBP plan offerings (Butler and Moffit, 1995; Cain, 1999). Several characteristics of the FEHBP design should make it vulnerable to adverse selection, including the large numbers of plan offerings and the absence of experience rating or risk adjustment in the government contributions to premiums. The information in Appendices C through L on plan offerings at the demonstration sites shows that benefits offered by FEHBP plans are fairly standardized but that premiums vary substantially across FEHBP plans, suggesting that risk selection indeed has occurred in FEHBP enrollments.

Aetna withdrew its indemnity plan from FEHBP in 1990, citing effects of adverse selection as the reason for leaving (Feldman, Dowd, and Coulam, 1999). Aetna's departure reduced the number of fee-for-service options, which may have contributed to the program's future stability. Fee-for-service plans are at greater risk of adverse selection because it is easier for people to switch among these options, compared with leaving HMO enrollment, which may involve having to switch physicians and other providers. Throughout the 1990s, the FEHBP has operated successfully, achieving low cost increases and avoiding premium spirals and financial damage for plans or beneficiaries that are symptomatic of adverse selection (Feldman, Dowd, and Coulam, 1999).

One of the factors that may be mitigating adverse selection in FEHBP is the structure of the government contribution to health plan premiums. The government pays 75 percent of any plan premium up to a specified "cap," a maximum that is established by legislation. The BBA replaced the previous formula for establishing the maximum with a "fair share" formula, in which the maximum is set at 72 percent of the enrollment weighted average of all premiums (Thorpe, Florence, and Gray, 1999). As discussed above, this varying government share should mitigate the severity of adverse selection pressures by making the plans with higher premiums relatively less costly for beneficiaries than they would be if the government paid a fixed dollar amount.

SECTION 4

HYPOTHESES FOR SELECTION BEHAVIORS IN FEHBP ENROLLMENTS

Selection dynamics for the FEHBP option involve two nested stages of selection behavior. The first stage is the decision to switch to FEHBP enrollment from another form of supplemental insurance. The second stage is the choice of a health plan, given the decision to enroll in FEHBP. Selection effects can be expected to occur at each stage, although it is not clear what the net direction of each effect will be, given the large number of combinations of originating and destination enrollment sectors.

Of note in this complex set of dynamics is the differing financial consequence when beneficiaries join an FEHBP HMO or a fee-for-service plan. According to the FEHBP rules (which apply to the DoD FEHBP demonstration), when a beneficiary enrolls in an FEHBP HMO, the HMO becomes primary payer and Medicare is the secondary payer. Medicare pays for services by fee-for-service providers if the beneficiary goes out of the FEHBP plan (in which case the beneficiary would be liable for the coinsurance), but it does not pay the copayments for the plan. When a beneficiary chooses an FEHBP fee-for-service plan, however, Medicare is the primary payer and the FEHBP plan picks up the coinsurance.

These coverage differences have differing consequences for beneficiaries who have Medicare Part B coverage and those who do not and, therefore, will affect their decisions regarding FEHBP enrollment. Medicare beneficiaries with Part B would obtain first dollar coverage if they enroll in an FEHBP *fee-for-service* plan, but those without Part B would have only partial coverage. The absence of Part B insurance would have weaker financial effects on beneficiaries in an FEHBP HMO because they would have full coverage by the HMO as long as they used providers in the HMO network. Higher-cost beneficiaries would be more likely to purchase Part B coverage and also would view richer benefit packages as appealing, especially if the FEHBP premium was lower than the costs of available Medigap policies or M+C plans in the local market.

Using the theoretical and empirical information presented in the previous section, we developed a set of hypotheses regarding expected enrollment and selection behaviors for Medicare-eligible DoD beneficiaries as they consider FEHBP as a supplemental insurance option. We believe that insurance decisions will differ substantially for those who have ready access to MTF direct-care services and those who do not. Beneficiaries residing in demonstration sites that contain MTF catchment areas will be less likely to select the FEHBP option because they would have to forgo utilization of MTF services as FEHBP enrollees. We also believe that beneficiaries who currently are enrolled in M+C plans will be less likely to choose the FEHBP option than those in fee-for-service Medicare. To access the FEHBP options, M+C plan enrollees would have to disenroll and return to fee for service, including the possible need to change providers, which involves larger transaction costs than switching supplemental insurance policies. Therefore, we have defined separate hypotheses for selection behavior based on proximity to MTF services as well as for the Medicare managed care and fee-for-service sectors. These hypotheses are presented below, followed by a summary in Table 5 of the factors hypothesized to influence FEHBP enrollment and related risk-selection effects.

ACCESS TO AND USE OF MTFS

The preference for military health care on the part of many retired career military personnel and their dependents is well documented, both through the advocacy activities of retiree associations and the apparent popularity of the newly available TRICARE Senior Prime demonstration. In addition, MTF care is financially attractive because there are no out-of-pocket costs for MTF services. Thus, one may presume that MTF direct-care services would be a strong competitor for FEHBP enrollment for beneficiaries in geographic proximity to these facilities. This presumption generates the following hypotheses regarding plan choice and associated selection effects.

1. The extent to which beneficiaries in MTF catchment areas will choose the FEHBP option will be inversely related to the amount of space-available care being provided by the MTF, because those with greater access to MTF direct-care services will be less likely to choose FEHBP.
2. In areas with MTFs that have medical education programs, there will be favorable selection into the FEHBP option because the MTF will be more likely to serve higher acuity (and higher cost) beneficiaries to support their teaching programs.
3. Overall enrollment rates in FEHBP will be lower in locations where TRICARE Senior Prime is available to beneficiaries (for the demonstration, Dover Air Force Base (AFB) represents this scenario) because some beneficiaries seeking DoD-sponsored benefits will prefer Senior Prime over FEHBP. However, all other factors being equal, the presence of Senior Prime will not necessarily lead to selection bias in FEHBP or other supplemental insurance options.
4. FEHBP enrollments for beneficiaries with no Part B coverage will be affected by the availability of MTF care because decisions by many military retirees to not enroll in Part B generally reflect their intentions to rely instead on MTF direct care. Beneficiaries without Part B coverage who reside in areas with no MTFs or with MTFs that have little space-available care will enroll in FEHBP at higher rates than other beneficiaries without Part B. These enrollment patterns will not involve adverse selection.

MANAGED CARE

Enrollees in M+C plans obtain full benefits from their health plans, including Medicare-covered benefits and supplemental benefits. Therefore, they will be comparing the full scope of benefits provided by their health plan, and the out-of-pocket costs they have incurred, to those offered in fee-for-service Medicare plus the FEHBP supplemental plan.

1. M+C plan enrollees with emerging serious health care needs are more likely than healthier enrollees to disenroll from the plan to return to fee-for-service Medicare, where they expect to have greater access to and choice of needed services. Most of these disenrollees will sign up for a supplemental insurance policy, with one of the choices being an FEHBP fee-for-service plan. Thus, FEHBP enrollees drawn from M+C plans as voluntary enrollees will be sicker and more costly than enrollees remaining in the M+C plans, contributing to adverse selection for FEHBP.
2. Involuntary M+C plan disenrollees because of withdrawals of health plans from Medicare are more likely than other plan enrollees to enroll in an FEHBP plan. The selection effects of switching plans will be adverse selection for FEHBP if the enrollees of discontinued plans are sicker and more costly than those enrolled in other M+C plans in the area.
3. Markets that have large numbers of beneficiaries enrolled in Medicare managed care or large numbers involuntarily disenrolled because of M+C plans exits will have the largest effects on the total size of enrollments into FEHBP from M+C plans. Associated selection effects identified in the previous two hypotheses will depend on the number and mix of beneficiaries involved in these large markets.

FEE FOR SERVICE

For fee-for-service beneficiaries, the FEHBP will be considered as an alternative to available Medigap insurance coverage. In this situation, FEHBP could be quite competitive financially if the federal contribution to premiums yields lower premium costs for beneficiaries. We expect that, if FEHBP were a permanent supplemental offering, beneficiaries would assess its value to them as one offering on a menu of Medigap options. Under demonstration conditions, however, many beneficiaries will be reluctant to take the risk of giving up a desirable insurance package without knowing if the new option will remain available.

1. As shown in the risk selection literature, the FEHBP options will experience adverse selection if they offer richer benefits for a higher price, compared with Medigap policies. If the prices are similar to or lower than Medigap policy prices, adverse selection effects will be smaller or may not occur.
2. Some beneficiaries who already have Medigap policies will be reluctant to drop the coverage for a demonstration, for fear of not being able to get equivalent coverage and prices later. Therefore, to attract enrollees for the demonstration, the FEHBP benefits will have to be richer than those for a permanent program, which could yield more severe FEHBP adverse selection in the demonstration than would occur for a permanent program, especially if prices also were higher.
3. Beneficiaries having supplemental coverage through employer group health retiree benefits will be reluctant to drop the coverage if their current premium and structure compares favorably to the FEHBP costs, in particular because many of the

employer-sponsored policies will not allow them to return after discontinuing the coverage.

4. FEHBP enrollments may be higher for DoD beneficiaries who are newly eligible for Medicare than for existing beneficiaries because they have not yet chosen to use M+C plans or stay in fee-for-service Medicare. New beneficiaries will be considering Medigap policies for the first time, including the FEHBP options, as they make these choices.

Table 5
Factors Hypothesized to Influence FEHBP Enrollments and Related Selection Effects

Explanatory Factor	Effect on FEHBP Enrollments	Selection Effect for FEHBP
Access to and use of MTFs		
1. Space-available care	Reduce	
2. MTF medical education	Reduce	Favorable
3. TRICARE Senior Prime site	Reduce	
4. Medicare Part B coverage	Increase	
Managed care enrollees		
1. Voluntary disenrollees due to poor health	Increase	Adverse
2. Involuntary disenrollees	Increase	
3. Size of health plan enrollment	Increase	
Fee-for-service beneficiaries		
1. Richness of FEHBP benefits	Increase	Adverse
2. Temporary status of demonstration	Reduce	
3. Employer group health benefits	Reduce	
4. Newly eligible for Medicare	Increase	
Good information		
1. Seekers of FEHBP information	Increase	Adverse
2. Number of options available	Decrease	

GOOD INFORMATION

Information is essential to effective enrollment decisions and also can influence adverse selection.

1. Beneficiaries have to know about the FEHBP options before they can choose this coverage, and those who are greater seekers of information will be more likely than others to be informed about the option. Adverse selection will occur for those who actively seek information because they will have the information to sort themselves across plans. It should not occur for those who do not gather and use this information. Therefore, net adverse effects will depend on what proportion of the population are users of information.

2. Having to choose from among a large number of plan options, including FEHBP, Medigap, and M+C plans, could discourage beneficiaries from participating in the FEHBP options because of the complexity of the decisions required. This effect is not likely to lead to adverse selection.

SECTION 5

A SUGGESTED METHODOLOGY TO EVALUATE SELECTION BIAS

With a set of hypotheses developed, the evaluation can proceed to define measures to analyze observed enrollment patterns in the demonstration and to test each hypothesis. In this section, we provide an overview of a suggested methodology and measures. Two basic policy questions should be the focus of these analyses:

1. To what extent does adverse selection occur in Medicare supplemental insurance enrollments for the DoD FEHBP demonstration?
2. If adverse selection is found to occur in FEHBP enrollment choices, how much does selection affect DoD health care costs for Medicare-eligible beneficiaries?

As we develop the approach, measures, and analytic methods to address these questions, we consider the availability of DoD data and any data constraints known to us. However, we do not address the more detailed measurement steps that will be necessary for a risk-selection analysis, such as coding variables and verifying data availability or designing primary data collection methods. This level of detail is beyond the scope of this study, which was intended to focus on the theoretical considerations of risk selection and their implications for designing a methodology to study selection effects appropriately for the DoD FEHBP demonstration.

OCCURRENCE OF SELECTION BIAS

To accomplish an effective analysis of the occurrence of selection bias, it will be necessary to characterize the enrollment choice properly and to perform the analysis with a carefully constructed set of variables that can test the hypotheses in Section 4. We first discuss the nature of the FEHBP enrollments as nested choices. Then we outline an analytic approach, a general model of enrollment as a function of several sets of factors, and the nature of the multivariate models that might be used. Finally, we list a set of variables that would be used as predictors in the enrollment choice analyses.

The Nested Enrollment Choice

The FEHBP enrollment choice consists of two stages: the decision to switch to FEHBP and the choice of plan within the FEHBP options. The factors that influence the first-level choice of switching to FEHBP may very well differ from those that influence the choice of plan within FEHBP. Therefore, the study needs to be designed to test effects at each stage of the FEHBP enrollment decision. One way to reduce the analytical burden would be to define the "within FEHBP" choices as either fee-for-service or HMO without attempting to measure the features of all the individual options. With this approach, however, it will be necessary to define aggregate measures at least for the premium costs of either type of option, given that price is well documented to be a primary driver of plan-switching behaviors.

Two other items need to be accommodated in specifying the analytic models and methods used to estimate risk selection effects. First, the number and types of health plans available to a beneficiary (the choice set) vary across geographic locations within the country. Second, newly eligible Medicare beneficiaries are making coverage choices under Medicare for the first time and are considering FEHBP along with all other options available to them, whereas beneficiaries already in Medicare are considering a decision to switch out of an existing plan to enroll in FEHBP. These two choices could be driven by quite different factors.

Because transaction costs rise with the number of choices (people need information on more options), enrollment rates may be diminished in markets with a larger number of options. In considering this issue, all possible coverage options must be considered, including not only the number of FEHBP options but also the number of M+C plans, Medigap plans, and Medicare SELECT plans, as well as the presence of Senior Prime.

Analytic Approaches

In analyses of the occurrence of selection bias, the two variables of policy interest are enrollment rates and the health status or relative risk of enrollees and non-enrollees. The health status or relative risk of each beneficiary is one of the determinants of his or her health benefit choices. Yet it is difficult to tease apart the independent influence of health status on these choices because of the interplay of multiple factors, which is amply illustrated by the hypotheses listed in Section 4. For effective analyses, the health status and relative risk measures need to be carefully defined and quantified so they can be interpreted with confidence. Ideally, the health status measures should be based on data for a point in time that is earlier than or coincides with the time of the benefit decision, to ensure that they can be interpreted as determinants of the benefit choice.

We recommend an approach that starts with descriptive statistics to become familiar with the patterns of FEHBP enrollments, the number and rates of enrollments that have occurred, average health status or relative risk measures, and variations across sites in all of these measures. Later in this section we discuss the measures that will be needed for the analysis. The information generated from the exploratory analysis should guide the approach to bivariate analyses and model specification for multivariate analyses. We note that only the multivariate analyses will yield the desired information on the independent effects of selection bias on FEHBP enrollments because it is through this modeling that the effects of other factors can be held constant. The choice of models will be complex and should be guided by theory as well as by any limitations in the available data.

Bivariate analyses. The bivariate analyses offer useful information in their own right on factors that appear to be influencing enrollment rates and selection bias, and they also provide guidance for ultimate specification of multivariate models. Some examples of useful bivariate comparisons include:

- Frequencies of FEHBP enrollment or not versus the following:
    - The presence of an MTF in the site or not.

- The beneficiary started in a fee-for-service or M+C plan.
- The beneficiary has supplemental insurance or not.

- Average values (and standard deviations) of health status or risk measures by resulting enrollment status in the FEHBP demonstration AND
  - the presence of an MTF in the site or not
  - enrollment status before decision (fee for service or M+C plan)
  - beneficiary has supplemental insurance or not.

Multivariate models. The modeling stage of the analysis will estimate models for enrollment probabilities in which coefficients on the health status variables represent the magnitude and direction of selection bias. As discussed in Section 2, according to utility theory, a consumer will make a health plan choice that will maximize utility. In the case of insurance choice, utility is a function of net income (or wealth) after insurance costs, the attractiveness of insurance benefits, and health status. Consumers will choose a plan to maximize their utility function. As shown in equation (1), for consumer *w* in market *y,* a plan choice P_{wy} can be modeled as a function of the factors that influence utility: consumer's health status h_{wy}, net income after insurance costs S_{wy}, current enrollment status E_{wy}, an array of characteristics of the plans in the market D_{my}, and an array of characteristics of the market M_y. Selection effects estimated by this equation include the main effect of health status (h_{wy}) as well as interaction effects of health status with plan characteristics ($h_{wy} D_{my}$) and market characteristics ($h_{wy} M_y$). The coefficients for the predictor variables are represented by τ_0-τ_3, ω_i, ϕ_k, β_j, and λ_l.

$$P_{wy} = \tau_0 + \tau_1 h_{wy} + \tau_2 S_{wy} + \tau_3 E_{wy} + \omega_i D_{my} + \phi_k M_y + \beta_j h_{wy} D_{my} + \lambda_l h_{wy} M_y \qquad (1)$$

Several models might be used to estimate effects on FEHBP enrollments, including a two-part model and a nested conditional logit model. The two-part model first estimates determinants of the probability of FEHBP enrollment, and then models determinants of the FEHBP plan choice for those who enrolled in FEHBP. This model assumes that a decision to enter FEHBP (the first part of the model) would not be affected by changes in the FEHBP options offered, which might not be the case if, say, a popular plan option were discontinued. The nested conditional logit model takes both steps of the decision process into account simultaneously by nesting the choice of FEHBP options within the basic FEHBP choice in the same model. The conditional nature of the model adjusts for differences in the number of plan choices available in different geographic areas.

It would be useful to estimate FEHBP enrollment models separately for beneficiaries who already were Medicare-eligible beneficiaries when the DoD FEHBP option was introduced and for those who had the FEHBP option available when they turned age 65 and made their initial plan enrollment decisions. The enrollment choices of new Medicare beneficiaries would represent the expected enrollment patterns and determinants of enrollment for FEHBP as an established option in a continuing program. By contrast, FEHBP enrollment rates for existing

Medicare beneficiaries might be suppressed by transaction costs that would dissuade them from switching out of existing plans.

Measures of Predictor Variables

The definition and measurement of specific variables within each of the predictor variable categories should be done with care to generate relevant and technically sound measures that can yield credible estimates of effects. We delineate many of the specific variables here, guided by the potential factors identified in the hypotheses. A menu of possible variables for analysis of selection bias in FEHBP is presented in Table 6, organized by predictor categories. It is not likely that all of these measures will be relevant, however, depending on the actual enrollment circumstances in the FEHBP demonstration. The measures listed are available from administrative data sources, with the exception of the set of measures on information availability and use, which typically are obtained from surveys. Some of the variables are readily measurable; others will require additional development before they can be used to estimate a model, and data inadequacies may preclude use of some measures. The intent of this listing is to identify the scope of items for future consideration in the evaluation of this demonstration program.

An unavoidable issue that researchers face in any risk selection analysis is the virtual impossibility of defining one standard health status measure to use as *the* risk selection predictor. Recognizing this reality, studies typically test more than one measure in their models. A variety of risk measures have been found to influence plan choice outcomes (or not), depending on the specific circumstances of the studies performed.

Three basic approaches are used to measure risk selection predictors: (1) abstraction of data on health status and health conditions from medical charts, (2) self-reported data on health status and health conditions collected in a survey, and (3) construction of relative risk measures based on diagnostic codes or service utilization records in administrative data. The remainder of this discussion assumes that only the second and third methods are options for this evaluation.

Our experience with using administrative data to measure relative risk, especially use of DoD direct-care data, leads us to advise caution in working with such measures. Availability of complete data for all beneficiaries is essential because missing data will introduce bias by underestimating the severity of health problems. This poses an issue for MTF direct-care data because outpatient encounters are known to be underreported in the Standard Ambulatory Data Record (SADR) data system, although completion rates have improved in the last 12 to 18 months. It should not be a problem for inpatient (SIDR) data, which have high completion rates.

Table 6
Measures to Be Used for Analyses of Selection Bias in FEHBP Enrollments

Category	Measures
Beneficiary characteristics	Age in 5-year age categories Gender Military retiree or family member Health status
Existing benefits coverage status	Part B coverage or not Plan enrollment status: Newly Medicare eligible and not yet in a plan M+C plan enrollee Senior Prime enrollee Fee-for-service Medicare, no supplemental coverage Fee-for-service Medicare, with Medigap Fee-for-service Medicare, with employer coverage Multiple supplemental policies
Access to an MTF	MTF capacity for space-available care (zero if no MTF) Medical education programs at MTF Ever use MTF direct-care services Extent of use of MTF direct-care services
FEHBP option characteristics	Only fee for service or also HMOs Number of FEHBP plans Premiums or cost sharing for FEHBP plans Extent of coverage for FEHBP plans
Other coverage options available	Presence of any M+C plans Number of M+C plans Presence of TRICARE Senior Prime Number of Medigap plans Number of Medicare SELECT plans
Site characteristics	Percentage of beneficiaries enrolled in M+C plans Location with involuntary M+C disenrollments M+C capitation rates
Information for decision process	Amount of information provided on FEHBP options Extent of knowledge about FEHBP

We list here some of the commonly used risk measures:

- Self-report of health status, four-point scale from excellent to poor.
- Self-report of functional status, using measures of activities of daily living.
- Self-reported SF-36 or SF-12 measures of physical and mental health status.
- Identification of presence or absence of each of a list of chronic conditions.
- Risk scores used for risk adjustment of capitation payments.

All of these measure except the last one typically are obtained from survey data (and some from chart abstraction). CMS has used 1999 inpatient claims and encounter data to establish risk scores for every Medicare beneficiary, which it is using to risk adjust M+C plan payments for 2000. These scores could be a useful risk selection measure for this evaluation.

EFFECTS OF SELECTION BIAS

To answer the policy question regarding the size of the cost effect of any selection bias in the DoD FEHBP option, it is necessary to decompose the cost effects of the demonstration into two components: (1) the change in DoD costs attributable to beneficiaries switching from their existing benefits to the FEHBP supplemental coverage, where the beneficiaries who switched to FEHBP had the same risk profile as those who did not switch, and (2) the change in DoD costs attributable to differences in the risk profiles of those who chose FEHBP and those who did not.

The DoD costs that need to be considered include costs of MTF direct-care services to the eligible population and costs for the federal share of the FEHBP premiums. For beneficiaries who enroll in FEHBP, costs will shift away from MTF direct-care costs to the FEHBP premium costs. At the same time, MTF direct-care costs may increase for other Medicare-eligible beneficiaries, to the extent that the departure of FEHBP enrollees opens up space-available care for others.

Risk selection will affect the FEHBP premium costs to the extent that these premiums are experience rated separately for the Medicare-eligible DoD beneficiaries, or if risk adjustments are added to premiums at some time in the future. Given the separate FEHBP risk pool established for Medicare-eligible DoD beneficiaries enrolled in FEHBP plans, this issue will become important as information on medical loss experiences accumulates for these enrollees. The larger FEHBP risk pool provides a cross-subsidy of costs across working and retired employees that is not available in the separate risk pool for the Medicare-eligible DoD enrollees. FEHBP plans can be expected to watch their medical care costs for the latter population and adjust premiums as necessary to cover expected costs. Therefore, DoD costs for premium contributions may change over time as a function of favorable or adverse selection among FEHBP enrollees. The FEHBP supplemental option also will affect the MTF direct-care costs, with the direction of effect depending on the risk profile of both the departing FEHBP enrollees and the remaining beneficiaries who continue to use the MTFs.

This discussion highlights the question of which comparison groups should be used when assessing the cost effects of risk selection for FEHBP enrollments in the demonstration. The choices should be guided by the policy questions of interest. As discussed above, two components of selection effects on DoD costs need to be considered. The first component is effects on DoD costs for FEHBP premium contribution, for which the appropriate comparison group is all other civilian FEHBP enrollees because the cap on the DoD contribution is based on the average costs for this group. The second component is effects on costs for MTF care obtained by Medicare-eligible DoD beneficiaries, for which other Medicare-eligible DoD beneficiaries using MTF care is the appropriate comparison group.

Two basic methods can be used to estimate the magnitude of risk selection effects on MTF direct-care costs. Whenever possible, we recommend both methods to test the robustness of the empirical results. These methods begin with person-level data records that contain the total costs for direct-care services used by the beneficiary, person-months of DoD eligibility, and a risk score calculated for the beneficiary, as well as other variables that will be used in the analyses. These methods are:

Comparisons of aggregate costs—With this method, direct-care costs and beneficiary-months of eligibility are summed within the groups that are being compared. The summations are performed in two ways. The first totals are the total actual costs and eligibility months, which yield estimates of total costs for all beneficiaries in a group and the average cost per beneficiary-month for the group. The other totals are total standardized costs and standardized costs per beneficiary-month, which are obtained by using the risk scores to adjust costs before aggregating the dollars. The difference between these two sets of costs represents the amount of costs attributable to risk selection.

Estimation of multivariate models of determinants of MTF costs—With this method, person-level data are used to estimate models in which total MTF care cost is the dependent variable and the risk score variable is a predictor variable along with variable(s) defining the comparison groups of interest and variables to control for other determinants of costs. Weighted models are estimated using months of eligibility as the weight, to obtain annualized cost estimates. When comparisons over time are of interest, a time series of cross-sections model could be used, for which the data file would contain a record for each person and each year of data being analyzed. For example, a model to compare MTF direct-care costs before and after initiating the demonstration would contain a record for a beneficiary's costs and characteristics for the baseline year and another record for the same beneficiary's costs in the year after introduction of FEHBP. Once a model is specified, the expected costs for groups with differing risk scores can be generated using the coefficients from the model.

We note that the validity of the MTF direct cost data will determine the quality of the information generated by either of these methods to estimate the cost effects of selection bias. Completion ratios for the SADR outpatient data will have to be used to account for the missing SADR records by adjusting the cost estimates upward. DoD derives completion ratios as the ratio of SADR record counts to Medical Expense and Performance Reporting System (MEPRS) workload counts of outpatient visits for each MTF, outpatient clinic, and month/year.

The other major measurement issue to be addressed is the method(s) for assigning costs to the SIDR inpatient care encounters and the SADR outpatient visits. This can be done by estimating unit costs for each inpatient ward and outpatient clinic within an MTF using the MEPRS data. This method yields estimates of the true DoD resource costs for delivering health care services. Alternatively, payment amounts could be simulated for each inpatient or outpatient encounter using either (a) the DoD payment system for network providers, (b) the DoD payment system for billing MTF services to third party payers, or (c) the Medicare payment system for inpatient and outpatient services. To the extent that resources permit, it would be informative to have comparison of costs estimated by several of these methods to provide a sensitivity analysis for the MTF resource cost estimates.

DISCUSSION

The information in this report was developed to provide a conceptual framework and methodological approach for consideration of risk selection issues in the evaluation of the DoD FEHBP demonstration. Drawing upon insurance theory as well as information on the supplemental insurance options available to Medicare beneficiaries, we examined the specific characteristics of the FEHBP option being tested for Medicare-eligible DoD beneficiaries and developed hypotheses regarding factors influencing enrollment choices and related risk selection. Then we developed a possible approach for an analysis of enrollment and risk selection, including potential models and predictor variables, to test the hypotheses and to estimate the cost effects of this program for DoD.

As stated several times in this report, the introduction of the FEHBP option as a demonstration can be expected to affect enrollments such that some of the observed enrollment or risk selection patterns cannot be generalized to the conditions of a permanent program. For example, sicker beneficiaries may be less likely to join a temporary program because they value the stability of their current providers and insurance coverage. Others may choose not to switch to FEHBP because they do not want to risk losing favorable premiums they have for their current Medigap insurance. Both of these examples argue for the value of a separate examination of enrollments for beneficiaries who are newly eligible for Medicare, who would be less likely to be affected by these factors than those who had established plans when FEHBP was introduced.

BIBLIOGRAPHY

AARP, *Public Policy Institute Issue Brief,* "Out-of-Pocket Spending on Health Care by Medicare Beneficiaries Age 65 and Older: 1999 Projections," publication ID: IB41, December 1999. Available at http://research.aarp.org/health/ib41_hspend.html (last accessed January 8, 2002).

Buchmueller, T. C., and P. J. Feldstein, "The Effect of Price on Switching Among Health Plans," *Journal of Health Economics,* 16:231–47, 1997.

Butler, S. M., and R. E. Moffit, "The FEHBP as a Model for a New Medicare Program," *Health Affairs*, 14(4):47–61, 1995.

Cain, H. P., II, "Moving Medicare to the FEHBP Model, or How to Make an Elephant Fly," *Health Affairs*, 18(4):25–39, 1999.

Castles, A., P. Goodwin, and C. Damberg, "Consumer Use of Quality of Care Information: An Evaluation of California Consumer HealthScope," *Abstract Book of the Association of Health Services Research,* Association for Health Services Research, Washington, D.C., 14:171–2, 1997.

Chernew, M., and D. P. Scanlon, "Health Plan Report Cards and Insurance Choice," *Inquiry* 35(1):9–22, 1998.

Christensen, S., and J. Shinogle, "Effects of Supplemental Coverage on Use of Services by Medicare Enrollees," *Health Care Financing Review*, 19(1):5–17, 1997.

Crofton, C., J. Lubalin, and C. S. Darby, "Foreword," *Medical Care* (Supplement) 37(3):S1–MS9, 1999.

Cutler, D. M., and S. Reber, *Paying for Health Insurance: The Tradeoff Between Competition and Adverse Selection*, National Bureau of Economic Research, Working Paper W5796, Cambridge, MA, October 1996.

Cutler, David M., and Richard J. Zeckhauser, *Adverse Selection in Health Insurance*, National Bureau of Economic Research, Working Paper 6107, Cambridge, MA, July 1997.

Cutler, David M., and Richard J. Zeckhauser, *Anatomy of Health Insurance*, National Bureau of Economic Research, Working Paper 7176, Cambridge, MA, June 1999.

Davis, K., K. Scott Collins, C. Schoen, and C. Morris, "Choice Matters: Enrollees' Views of Their Health Plans," *Health Affairs,* 14(2):99–112, 1995.

Dowdal, T., W. Hamilton, J. Baugher, M. Fisher, F. Foley, R. Hultgren, S. Jones, and M. Stepek, "Health Insurance for the Elderly: Owning Duplicate Policies is Costly and Unnecessary," General Accounting Office, Washington, D.C., 1994.

Etheredge, L. "Purchasing Medicare Prescription Drug Benefits: A New Proposal," *Health Affairs*, 18:7–19, 1999.

Ettner, S. L. "Adverse Selection and the Purchase of Medigap Insurance by the Elderly," *Journal of Health Economics,* 16:543–62, 1997.

Farley, D. O., P. F. Short, M. N. Elliott, D. E. Kanouse, J. A. Brown, and R. D. Hays, "Effects of CAHPS® Health Plan Performance Information on Plan Choices by New Jersey Medicaid Beneficiaries," *Health Services Research,* in press.

Feldman, R., C. Escribano, and L. Pellise, "The Role of Government in Health Insurance Markets with Adverse Selection," *Health Economics,* 7:659–70, 1998.

Feldman, R., B. Dowd, and R. Coulam, "The Federal Employees Health Benefits Plan: Implications for Medicare Reform," *Inquiry,* 36:189–199, 1999.

Feldman, R., J. Christianson, and J. Schultz, "Do Consumers Use Information to Choose a Health-Care Provider System?" *Milbank Quarterly*, 78(1):47–77, 2000.

Frank, R. G., J. Glazer, and T. G. McGuire, *Measuring Adverse Selection in Managed Health Care*, National Bureau of Economic Research, Working Paper 6825, Cambridge, MA, December 1998.

Gertler, P. J., R. Sturm, and B. Davidson, *Information and the Demand for Supplemental Medicare Insurance*, National Bureau of Economic Research, Working Paper 4700, Cambridge, MA, April 1994.

Gibbs, D. A., J. A. Sangl, and B. Burrus, "Consumer Perspectives on Information Needs for Health Plan Choice," *Health Care Financing Review,* 18:55–73, 1996.

Gross, D. and N. Brangan, "Out-of-Pocket Spending on Health Care by Medicare Beneficiaries Age 65 and Older: 1999 Projections," *AARP Public Policy Institute Issue Brief*, IB#41, December 1999. Obtained from AARP web site (www.aarp.org).

Health Care Financing Administration, *Medicare+Choice Changes for the Year 2000*, November 1999a. Obtained from CMS web site (www.hcfa.gov).

Health Care Financing Administration, *Medicare and You 2000,* 1999b. Obtained from CMS web site (www.medicare.gov).

Health Care Financing Administration, *2000 Guide to Health Insurance for People with Medicare,* March 2000. Obtained from CMS web site (www.medicare.gov).

Kaiser Foundation, *The Medicare Program: Medicare at a Glance,* September 1999. Obtained from web site (www.kff.org).

Kanouse, D. E., M. E. Spranca, J. Uhrig, M. N. Elliott, P. F. Short, D. O. Farley, and R. D. Hays, *Effects of CAHPS Reports on Medicaid Recipients' Choice of Health Plans in a Laboratory Setting,* paper presented at the meeting of the Association for Health Services Research, Los Angeles, CA, 2000.

Khandker, R. K., and L. A. McCormack, "Medicare Spending by Beneficiaries with Various Types of Supplemental Insurance," *Medical Care Research Review,* 56:137–55, 1999.

Knutson, D. J., N. Dahms, E. Kind, J. McGee, M. Finch, and J. B. Fowles, "The Effect of Health Plan Report Cards on Consumer Knowledge, Attitudes and Plan Choice: A Quasi-

Experimental Evaluation," *Abstracts of the Association of Health Service Research,* Association of Health Services Research, Washington, D.C., 14:184, 1997.

Langwell, K., et al., *Analysis of Benefits Offered by Medicare HMOs, 1999: Complexities and Implications*, prepared by the Barents Group LLC for the Kaiser Family Foundation, August 1999. Obtained from web site (www.kff.org).

Lillard, L. A., and J. Rogowski, *Does Supplemental Private Insurance Increase Medicare Costs?* RAND, DRU-477-RC, Santa Monica, CA, 1995.

Lillard, L. A., J. Rogowski, and R. Kington, *Insurance Coverage for Prescription Drugs: Effects on Use and Expenditures in the Medicare Population,* RAND, DRU-2073-NIA, Santa Monica, CA, 1999.

Lillard, L., J. Rogowski, and R. Kington, "Long-Term Determinants of Patterns of Health Insurance Coverage in the Medicare Population," *Gerontologist,* 37:314–23, 1997.

Manning, W. G., and M. S. Marquis, "Health Insurance: The Tradeoff Between Risk Pooling and Moral Hazard," *Journal of Health Economics*, 15:609–639, 1996.

Marquis, M. S., "Adverse Selection with a Multiple Choice Among Health Insurance Plans: A Simulation Analysis," *Journal of Health Economics,* 11:129–51, 1992.

Marquis, M. S., and J. L. Buchanan, "Simulating the Effects of Employer Contributions on Adverse Selection and Health Plan Choice," *Health Services Research,* 34:813–37, 1999.

Marquis, M. S., and M. R. Holmer, "Alternative Models of Choice Under Uncertainty and Demand for Health Insurance," *The Review of Economics and Statistics*, 78(3):421–427, 1996.

Marquis, M. S., and J. A. Rogowski, *Participation in Alternative Health Plans,* RAND, R-4105-HCFA, Santa Monica, CA, 1991.

McCormack, L. A., P. D. Fox, T. Rice, and M. L. Graham, "Medigap Reform Legislation of 1990: Have the Objectives Been Met?" *Health Care Financing Review,* 18:157–74, 1996.

Mechanic, D., T. Ettel, and D. Davis, "Choosing Among Health Insurance Options: A Study of New Employees," *Inquiry,* 27:14–23, 1990.

Neipp, J., and R. Zeckhauser, "Persistence in the Choice in Health Plans," R. M. Scheffler and L. F. Rossiter, eds., *Advances in Health Economics and Health Services Research,* Vol. 6, JAI Press, Greenwich, CT, pp. 2–44, 1985.

O'Connell, J. M., "Determinants of Medical Spending by the Elderly: The Importance of Medicare Supplemental Insurance," *AHSR Annual Meeting Abstracts,* AHSR, Washington, D.C., 1996.

Office of Personnel Management, *The Federal Employees Health Benefits Program and Medicare*, November 1999 (RI 75-12). Obtained from the OPM web site (www.opm.gov).

Office of Personnel Management, *FEHB Program Handbook for Enrollees and Employing Offices.* Obtained from the OPM web site (www.opm.gov).

Physician Payment Review Commission (PPRC), *1996 Annual Report to Congress*, Washington D.C., 1996.

Robinson, S., and M. Brodie, "Understanding the Quality Challenge for Health Consumers: The Kaiser/AHCPR Survey," *Joint Commission Journal on Quality Improvement,* 23(5):239–44, 1997.

Sainfort, F., and B. C. Booske, "Role of Information in Consumer Selection of Health Plans," *Health Care Financing Review,* 18(1):31–54, 1996.

Scanlon, D. P., M. Chernew, and J. R. Lave, "Consumer Health Plan Choice: Current Knowledge and Future Directions," *Annual Review of Public Health,* 18:507–28, 1997.

Spranca, M. E., D. E. Kanouse, P. F. Short, D. O. Farley, and R. D. Hays, "Do Consumer Reports of Health Plan Quality Affect Health Plan Selection?" *Health Services Research*, 35:933–947, 2000.

Stuart, B., and J. Grana, "Are Prescribed and Over-the-Counter Medicines Economic Substitutes? A Study of the Effects of Health Insurance on Medicine Choices by the Elderly," *Medical Care,* 33:487–501, 1995.

Taylor, A. K., P. J. Farley, and C. M. Horgan, "Medigap Insurance: Friend or Foe in Reducing Medicare Deficits?" H. E. Frech III, ed., *Health Insurance: Public or Private,* Pacific Institute for Public Policy Research, San Francisco, CA, 1988.

Thorpe, K. F., C. S. Florence, and B. Gray, "Market Incentives, Plan Choice, and Price Increases," *Health Affairs*, 18(6):194–202, 1999.

Tumlinson, A., H. Bottigheimer, P. Mahoney, E. M. Stone, and A. Hendricks, "Choosing a Health Plan: What Information Will Consumers Use?" *Health Affairs,* 16:229–38, 1997.

"Uniformed Services Retirees' Federal Employees Health Benefits Program Demonstration: Most Frequently Asked Questions," December 17, 1999. Obtained from web site (www.tricare.osd.mil/fehbp/FAQ).

Van de Ven, W.P.M.M., and R.C.J.A. Van Vliet, "Consumer Information Surplus and Adverse Selection in Competitive Health Insurance Markets: An Empirical Study," *Journal of Health Economics,* 14:149–169, 1995.

Vistnes, J. P., and J. S. Banthin, "The Demand for Medicare Supplemental Insurance Benefits: The Role of Attitudes Toward Medical Care and Risk," *Inquiry,* 34:311–24, 1997.

Wolfe, J. R., and J. H. Goddeeris, "Adverse Selection, Moral Hazard, and Wealth Effects in the Medigap Insurance Market," *Journal of Health Economics,* 10:433–459, 1991.

Appendix A

Nationwide Medicare and FEHBP Plan Coverage

Table A.1
Medicare Benefits and Cost-Sharing Requirements, 2000

Services	Beneficiary Cost-Sharing
Hospital Insurance Program (Part A)	
Inpatient Hospital Care	Deductible: $776 per inpatient hospital episode. No coinsurance for first 60 days. $194 a day coinsurance for the 61st-90th days. $388 a day for 60 lifetime reserve days.
Skilled Nursing Facility	No coinsurance for the first 20 days; $97 coinsurance per day for the 21st-100th days.
Post-institutional Home Health Care	No coinsurance.
Hospice Care	Nominal coinsurance for outpatient drugs and inpatient respite care. HI premium $39.
Supplementary Medical Insurance Program (Part B)	
Premium and Deductible	2000 Premium: $45.50 per month (=$525.60 per year). Deductible: $100 per year.
Physician and Other Medical Services	Coinsurance of 20% of the approved amount. Additional charges of up to 15% of the approved amount for non-participating physician services.
Outpatient Hospital Care	20% coinsurance of approved amount.
Ambulatory Surgical Services	20% coinsurance.
Clinical Diagnostic Laboratory Services	No coinsurance.
Outpatient Mental Health Services	50% coinsurance of the approved amount for psychotherapy, and 20% for medical management.
Home Health Care (other than post-institutional)	No coinsurance.
Durable Medical Equipment	20% coinsurance of approved amount.
Preventive Services (subject to frequency schedules)	
• Screening mammograms	No deductible; 20% coinsurance of the approved amount.
• Pelvic and clinical breast exams	No deductible; 20% coinsurance.
• Screening Pap smear	No deductible or coinsurance.
• Screening tests for colorectal cancer (fecal occult blood test; colonoscopy; etc.)	Cost sharing varies depending on the specific procedure involved.
• Glucose monitoring for beneficiaries with diabetes (as of July 1, 1998)	20% coinsurance.
• Diabetes education (as of July 1, 1998)	20% coinsurance.
• Bone mass measurement (July 1, 1998)	20% coinsurance.
• Flu and pneumococcal vaccines	No deductible or coinsurance.

Table A.2
Nationwide FEHBP Plans

Plan Name	Benefit Type	Calendar Year	Prescription Drugs	Per Stay Inpatient	Catastrophic Limit	Doctors	Outpatient Tests	Room & Board	Other	Outpatient	Generic	Brand	Self Only	Self and Family
Plans open to all:														
Alliance Health Plan	PPO	$100*	$200C*	$150	$2,000*	10%	10%	10%	10%	10%	20%	20%	207.83	421.39
	Non-PPO	$300*	$200C*	$250	$3,000*	30%	30%	30%	30%	30%	20%	20%		
APWU Health Plan	PPO	$250	$50L	None	$2,000	10%	10%	10%	10%	10%	$7	$25	129.65	278.07
	Non-PPO	$250	$50L	$200	$3,500	30%	30%	30%	30%	30%	$7	$25		
Blue Cross Blue Shield—High	PPO	$150	None	None	$1,000	5%	5%	0	0	$10	$8	$14	143.63	
	Non-PPO	$150	None	$100	$2,700	20%	20%	30%	30%	$100/d	$8	$14		291.09
Blue Cross Blue Shield—Standard	PPO	$200	None	None	$2,000	10%	10%	0	0	$25	$12	$20		
	Non-PPO	$200	None	$250	$3,750	25%	25%	30%	30%	$150/d	$12	$20	65.09	144.69
GEHA Benefit Plan	PPO	$300	None	None	$2,500	10%	10%	0	10%	10%	$10	$30		
	Non-PPO	$300	None	None	$3,500	25%	25%	0	25%	25%	$10	$30	99.06	200.78
Mail Handlers—High	PPO	$150	$250C*	None	$2,500	10%	10%	0	0	10%	$10	$30		
	Non-PPO	$150	$250C*	$250	$4,000	30%	30%	0	0	30%	$10	$45	95.98	234.32
Mail Handlers—Standard	PPO	$200	$600C*	$150	$4,000	10%	10%	0	0	10%	$10	$40		
	Non-PPO	$200	$600C*	$300	$4,000	30%	30%	0	0	30%	$10	$55	70.63	175.85
NALC	PPO	$275	$25L	None	$3,000	15%	15%	0	0	15%	$12	$25		
	Non-PPO	$275	$25L	$100	$3,500	30%	30%	20%	20%	30%	$12	$25	128.81	258.98
Postmasters—High	PPO	$200	$50	None	$2,500	10%	10%	0	0	10%	$5	$12		
	Non-PPO	$275	$100	$150	$2,500	15%	20%	0	15%	20%	$5	$12	286.43	605.26
Postmasters—Standard	PPO	$200	$50	None	$3,000	10%	10%	0	0	10%	$10	$20		
	Non-PPO	$350	$100	$250	$4,500	30%	30%	30%	30%	30%	$10	$20	174.07	364.74

NOTES: Some plans apply a separate deductible to the combined purchase of mail order drugs and drugs from local pharmacies (C), while others apply it to drugs purchased from local pharmacies only (L). Some plans (*) require each family member to meet a per person deductible.

Appendix B

Theoretical Model of Health Plan Offerings

THEORETICAL MODEL OF HEALTH PLAN OFFERINGS

The choices by DoD beneficiaries of supplemental health insurance coverage involve market interactions between these consumer choices and the insurance offerings of other important market participants: the health plans being offered and the purchasers offering those plans. The objectives and relationships of these market participants are summarized in this model, and details of this theoretical framework are presented in Figure B.1.

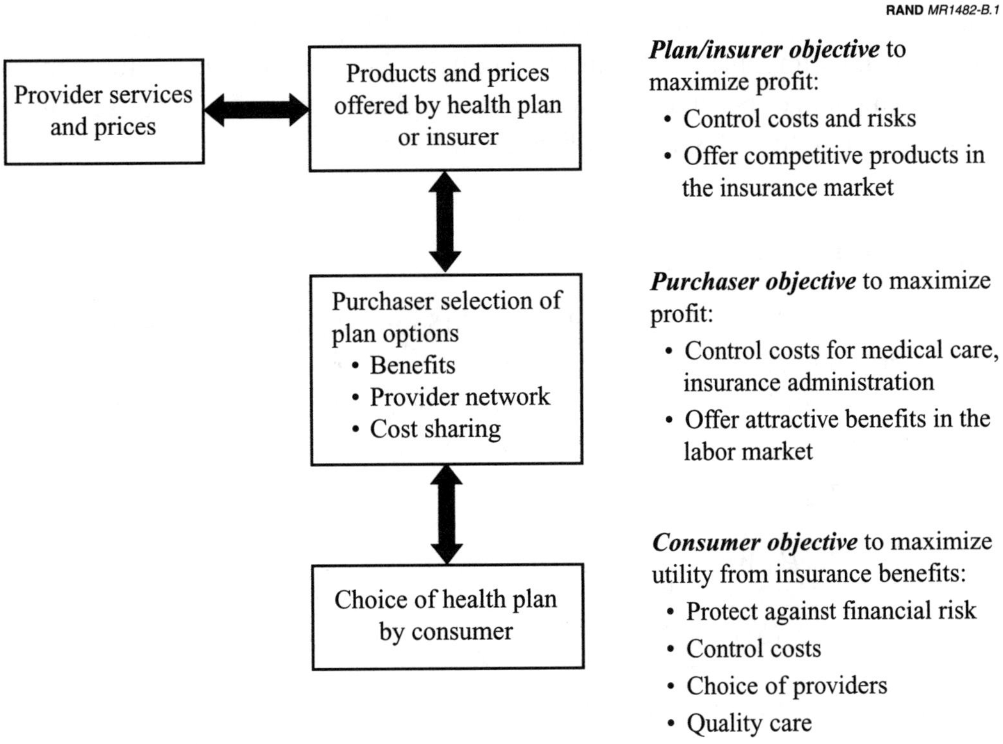

Figure B.1—Participants in a Health Insurance Market

THE HEALTH PLAN/INSURER PERSPECTIVE

We look first at the factors considered by a health plan or insurer when structuring its insurance offerings. The total profit θ of a health plan or insurance intermediary is the difference between its total revenue across all insurance products i sold to purchasers j and its costs to provide those services, E_i. As shown in equation (B.1), the revenue for each product is the product price p_{ij} multiplied by the number of workers w_{ij} who choose that product. The factors that will determine w_{ij}, represented in equation (B.2), are (1) the price and other features f_{ikj} of the health plan's product i at firm j, and (2) the price and other features g_{ckj} of competing insurance products. Expense for each product, shown in equation (B.3), is the sum of costs for medical care q_i, administrative costs a_i, and costs associated with establishing the level of product quality

z_i. We assume that these expenses do not vary when the same product is sold to different purchasers, although the premiums charged may vary.

$$\theta = \sum_{ij} p_{ij} w_{ij} - \sum_{i} E_i \tag{B.1}$$

$$w_{ij} = \alpha_j p_{ij} + \phi_{kj} f_{ikj} + \gamma_j p_{cj} + \delta_{kj} g_{ckj} \tag{B.2}$$

$$E_i = \beta_0 + \beta_1 q_i + \beta_2 a_i + \beta_3 z_i \tag{B.3}$$

When structuring its products and prices, the insurer considers the size and direction of the unit cost coefficients on each insurance feature. An insurer's benefits packages must be competitive in the market and affordable for the insurer to offer. The insurer will structure the packages to be attractive to purchasers and consumers, while setting prices in a way to control adverse selection that would lead to high service utilization (q_i) and associated escalation of costs ($B_1 q_i$).

THE PURCHASER'S PERSPECTIVE

A firm's profit, π, on its product Q for price P, is the difference between its revenue and the costs to generate the product. As shown in equation (B.4), we represent the costs as having four components: per-worker cost for salaries S for the firm's workers W, per-worker benefit costs B, per-unit supply and material cost C, and fixed costs of capital F.

$$\pi = PQ - (SW + BW + CQ + F) \tag{B.4}$$

$$BW = \sum_{m} p_m w_m - \sum_{m} r_m w_m + A \tag{B.5}$$

$$W = f(U_e(S(1 - r_m), I(h_e), O), U_a) \tag{B.6}$$

The benefits cost, BW, is represented by equation (B.5). The firm chooses to offer a number of health plan options, m, for which the firm pays premiums p_m and incurs administrative costs A to manage all the health insurance benefits. The number of workers enrolling in each plan is represented by w_m. To maximize profit, the firm wishes to minimize BW (subject to the constraint of workers' insurance preferences), which it may do by negotiating benefits packages and premium p with the health plans, or by sharing the premium cost with the workers. The reduction in cost for the firm associated with the workers' share of premium, r, is shown in the second term of equation (B.5). The design of the firm's and each worker's share of the premium and other cost sharing will influence plan choices and resulting adverse selection issues, which we discuss in the next subsection.

Equation (B.6) represents the competitive position of the firm in the labor market. The number of qualified workers W that the firm attracts is a function of the utility, U_e, derived by potential workers for joining firm e, where workers will choose firm e when $U_e > U_a$ for other firm options. U_e is a function of the net salary offered $S(1\text{-}r_m)$, attractiveness of health insurance benefits I, and other features of employment, O. The term $(1\text{-}r_m)$ is the proportion of salary remaining after each worker's share of the health insurance premium for plan *m*. The terms $I(h_e)$ defines the attractiveness of the benefits as a function of each worker's health status.

Only equation (B.5) is relevant for governmental purchasers like Medicare or TRICARE because governmental organizations are concerned about cost but not about profits or attracting beneficiaries to the program. It is useful, however, to rewrite equation (B.6) to reflect the government's position in offering plan options that are of value to the beneficiaries, which we present in equation (B.7). Here, the number of beneficiaries *b* who enroll in plan *m* is a function of the utility, U_m, derived by potential joining plan *m*, where beneficiaries choose plan *m* when $U_m > U_a$ for other plan options. U_e is a function of the beneficiary's net income $S(1-r_m)$, the attractiveness of health insurance benefits *I,* and health status *H*.

$$w_m = f(U_e(S(1-r_m), I(h_m), H), U_a) \tag{B.7}$$

When integrating the preferences of consumers into their health insurance product decisions, health plans and purchasers must estimate both consumers' preferences and health status, often with incomplete information. Selection may arise when there is asymmetric information about consumers' health status (i.e., the consumer knows he or she has high health care needs but the plan does not). As we discuss below, without sufficient information, plans may establish premiums and cost-sharing provisions that segment plan enrollments between the more costly and less costly consumers, thus leading to cost escalation and market failures.

THE CONSUMER'S PERSPECTIVE

Consumers in the workforce make choices at two levels that involve evaluation of the health plan options available to them. First, consumers consider the health benefits offered by potential employers when seeking employment in the labor market. Then, once an individual has become a worker for a firm, or is retired and a Medicare beneficiary, the utility of health benefits plays a role in his or her health plan choice. According to utility theory, a consumer makes a health plan choice that will maximize utility, which is a function of net income (or wealth) after insurance costs, the attractiveness of insurance benefits, and health status, as given by equation (B.8). This utility function is operationalized in the actual choice of plan M_w by a consumer, which is determined by the consumer's health status h_w, net income $S(1-r_m)$, and an array of plan characteristics D_m, as shown by equation (B.9).

$$Max\, U_e(S(1-r_m), I(h_m), H) \tag{B.8}$$

$$M_w = \tau_0 + \tau_1 h_w + \tau_2 S_w(1-r_m) + \tau_3 D_m \tag{B.9}$$

Two important factors in consumer health plan choices are inherent to any insurance market. First, the consumer preferences that guide their choices of health benefits drive many of the performance outcomes of insurance suppliers and group purchasers. These consumer preferences are taken into account by insurers as they design the options they offer, as well as by group purchasers as they select the set of plans they will offer to their employees or beneficiaries. Second, the insurers and purchasers face financial uncertainty with respect to how many people will enroll in each plan, as well as to how costly their health care utilization will be.

When insurers and purchasers face high financial risk due to heterogeneity in consumers' health status, or uncertainty in the information available to them, they will configure benefit structures, premiums, and cost-sharing provisions to reduce that risk.

APPENDIX C

ADAIR, IOWA

(includes all of Iowa outside MTF catchment area and parts of Minnesota, South Dakota, Nebraska, Kansas, and Missouri outside MTF catchment areas)

1) **Map of Demonstration Area**
2) **Summary of Local FEHBP Options**
3) **Summary of Medicare+Choice Options**

FEHBP Demonstration: Adair, Iowa

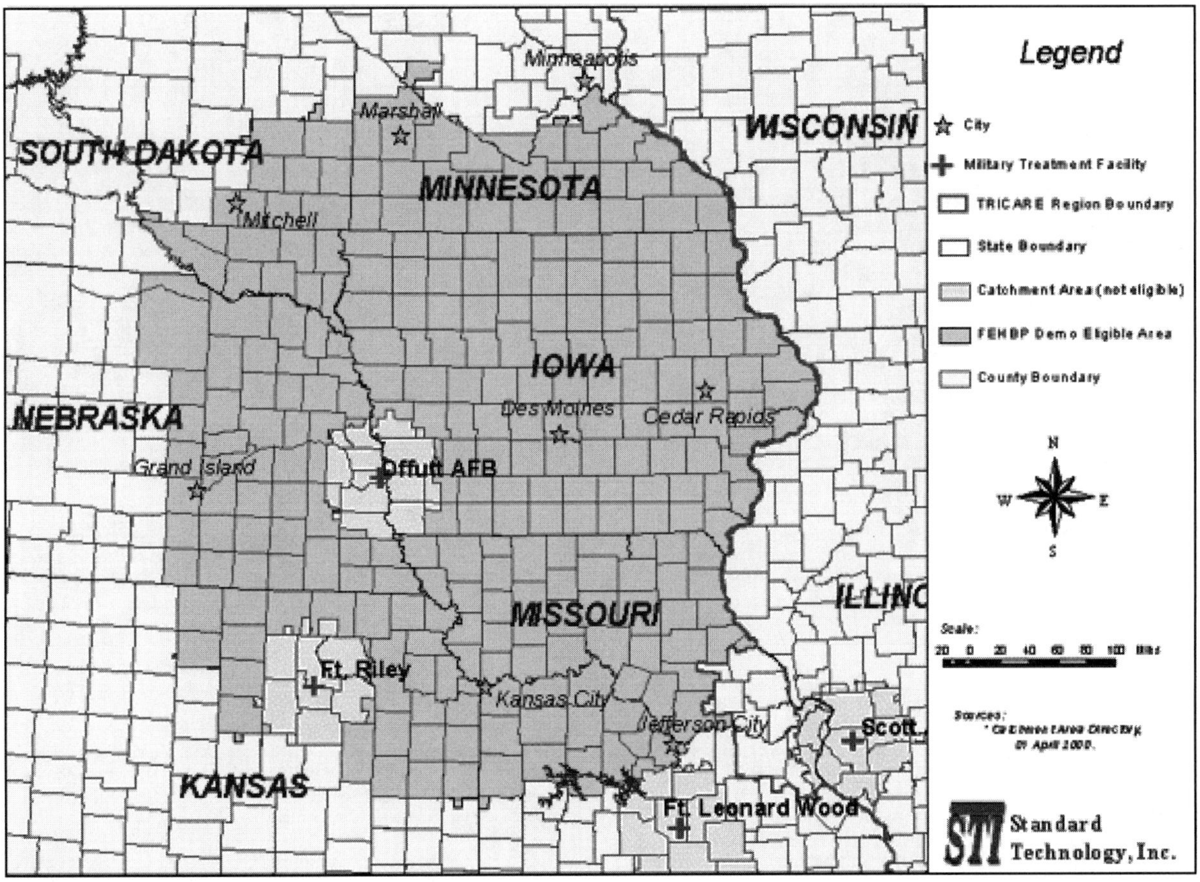

Adair, Iowa FEHBP Options

POS									
APWU Health Plan Minneapolis/St. Paul									
Monthly		Primary care doctor	Hospital room copay/ insurance	Prescription drugs, generic	Prescription drugs, brand	Primary care doctor office copay	Hospital inpatient R&B charges	Prescription drugs, generic	R/Brand/ Local
Self only	Self & family								
premium		In Network You Pay				Out of Network You Pay			
129.65	278.07	$10	0	20%	20%	30%	30%	40%	40%
Blue Cross and Blue Shield-Std All of Minnesota									
Monthly		Primary care doctor	Hospital room copay/ insurance	Prescription drugs, generic	Prescription drugs, brand	Primary care doctor office copay	Hospital inpatient R&B charges	Prescription drugs, generic	R/Brand/ Local
Self only	Self & family								
premium		In Network You Pay				Out of Network You Pay			
65.09	144.69	$10	0	$5	$15	25%	30%	45%	45%
Blue Cross and Blue Shield-Std Most of Kansas									
Monthly		Primary care doctor	Hospital room copay/ insurance	Prescription drugs, generic	Prescription drugs, brand	Primary care doctor office copay	Hospital inpatient R&B charges	Prescription drugs, generic	R/Brand/ Local
Self only	Self & family								
premium		In Network You Pay				Out of Network You Pay			
65.09	144.69	$10	0	$5	$15	25%	30%	45%	45%

GEHA Benefit Plan Omaha area		Primary care doctor	Hospital room copay/ insurance	Prescription drugs, generic	Prescription drugs, brand	Primary care doctor office copay	Hospital inpatient R&B charges	Prescription drugs, generic	R/Brand/ Local
Monthly									
Self only	Self & family								
premium		In Network You Pay				Out of Network You Pay			
99.06	200.78	$10	0	$5	$15	25%	0	$5	$15

Adair, Iowa FEHBP Quality Ratings

	Satisfaction Indicators 1=above average, 2=average, 3=below average							
Plan Name	Overall plan satisfaction	Getting needed care	Getting care quickly	How well doctors communicate	Courteous and helpful office staff	Customer service	Claims processing	Child survey Overall satisfactoin
APWU Health Plan Minneapolis/St. Paul	1	1	2	2	1	1	1	1
Blue Cross and Blue Shield-Std All of Minnesota	2	3	3	2	2	2	1	2
Blue Cross and Blue Shield-Std Most of Kansas	2	3	3	2	2	2	1	2
GEHA Benefit Plan Omaha area	3	2	2	2	2	2	3	3

MINNESOTA/SOUTH DAKOTA/NEBRASKA/KANSAS/MISSOURI MEDICARE HEALTH PLAN COMPARISONS

	Coventry Health Care Of Iowa, Inc. (H1653 - 002) Central Iowa	**John Deere Health Plan, Inc.** Senior Care Basic (H1472 - 001) Iowa	**John Deere Health Plan, Inc.** Senior Care Choice (H1472 - 002) Iowa	**Medical Associates Health Plan, Inc.** (H1651 - 001) Iowa	**Medical Associates Health Plan, Inc.** (H1651 - 002) Iowa
Premium (Part B - $45.50/month in 2000)		You pay $109 a month if you have Medicare Parts A and B.	You pay $150 a month if you have Medicare Parts A and B.		
Physician Visits		You pay $10 for each visit with your personal physician.	You pay $10 for each visit with your personal physician.		
Inpatient Hospital		You pay $250 for each admission to a plan hospital. You are covered for additional days in the hospital. Contact plan for details.	You pay nothing for your hospital stay. You are covered for additional days in the hospital. Contact plan for details.		
Doctor Choice		You need a referral to see a specialist, except for your annual GYN visit.	You need a referral to see a specialist, except for your annual GYN visit.		

	Coventry Health Care Of Iowa, Inc. (H1653 - 002) Central Iowa	**John Deere Health Plan, Inc.** Senior Care Basic (H1472 - 001) Iowa	**John Deere Health Plan, Inc.** Senior Care Choice (H1472 - 002) Iowa	**Medical Associates Health Plan, Inc.** (H1651 - 001) Iowa	**Medical Associates Health Plan, Inc.** (H1651 - 002) Iowa
Prescription Drugs		You pay 100% for most prescription drugs.	Prescription drugs are covered with limits. You pay $7 per generic prescription. You pay $7 per brand name prescription. Your generic and brand name prescription drugs are covered up to $600 per year. You must use plan-approved prescription drugs. There are other limits on prescription drugs. Contact plan for details.		
Physical Exams		You pay $10 for a physical exam. You are covered for 1 physical exam(s) per year.	You pay $10 for a physical exam. You are covered for 1 physical exam(s) per year.		
Vision Services		Routine eye exams and glasses are not covered. You are covered for diagnostic and therapeutic services for the eye.	You have some coverage for glasses and routine eye exams. Contact plan for details.		
Dental		In general, you pay 100% for dental services.	In general, you pay 100% for dental services.		

MINNESOTA/SOUTH DAKOTA/NEBRASKA/KANSAS/MISSOURI MEDICARE HEALTH PLAN COMPARISONS (cont.)

	Sioux Valley Health Plan Basic Plan (H4349 - 002) SD/Iowa	**Sioux Valley Health Plan** Plus Plan (H4349 - 003) SD/Iowa	**United Healthcare of the Midlands, Inc.** Medicare Complete--Omaha/Council Bluffs (H2802 - 001) Nebraska	**First Plan of Minnesota** First Plan of Minnesota (H2461 - 001)	**Healthpartners** (H2462 - 999) Minneapolis/St. Paul
Premium (Part B - $45.50/month in 2000)	You pay $49 a month if you have Medicare Parts A and B.	You pay $99 a month if you have Medicare Parts A and B.	You pay nothing if you have Medicare Parts A and B.		
Physician Visits	You pay $10 for each visit with your personal physician.	You pay $10 for each visit with your personal physician.	You pay $15 for each visit with your personal physician.		
Inpatient Hospital	You pay nothing for your hospital stay. You are covered for additional days in the hospital. Contact plan for details.	You pay nothing for your hospital stay. You are covered for additional days in the hospital. Contact plan for details.	You are covered for additional days in the hospital. Contact plan for details.		
Doctor Choice	You do not need a referral to see a specialist.	You do not need a referral to see a specialist.	You need a referral to see a specialist some of the time. Contact plan for details.		

	Sioux Valley Health Plan Basic Plan (H4349 - 002) SD/Iowa	**Sioux Valley Health Plan** Plus Plan (H4349 - 003) SD/Iowa	**United Healthcare of the Midlands, Inc.** Medicare Complete--Omaha/Council Bluffs (H2802 - 001) Nebraska	**First Plan of Minnesota** First Plan of Minnesota (H2461 - 001)	**Healthpartners** (H2462 - 999) Minneapolis/St. Paul
Prescription Drugs	You pay 100% for most prescription drugs.	Prescription drugs are covered with limits. You pay $10 per generic prescription. You pay $20 per brand name prescription. Your generic and brand name prescription drugs are covered up to $1,000 per year. There is a monthly limit for prescription drugs. Contact plan for details.	You pay 100% for most prescription drugs.		
Physical Exams	You pay nothing for a physical exam. You are covered for 1 physical exam(s) per year.	You pay nothing for a physical exam. You are covered for 1 physical exam(s) per year.	You pay $15 for a physical exam. You are covered for 1 physical exam(s) per year.		
Vision Services	You have some coverage for glasses, contacts and routine eye exams. Contact plan for details.	You have some coverage for glasses, contacts and routine eye exams. Contact plan for details.	You have some coverage for routine eye exams. Contact plan for details.		

	Sioux Valley Health Plan Basic Plan (H4349 - 002) SD/Iowa	**Sioux Valley Health Plan** Plus Plan (H4349 - 003) SD/Iowa	**United Healthcare of the Midlands, Inc.** Medicare Complete--Omaha/Council Bluffs (H2802 - 001) Nebraska	**First Plan of Minnesota** First Plan of Minnesota (H2461 - 001)	**Healthpartners** (H2462 - 999) Minneapolis/St. Paul
Dental	In general, you pay 100% for dental services.	In general, you pay 100% for dental services.	In general, you pay 100% for dental services.		

MINNESOTA/SOUTH DAKOTA/NEBRASKA/KANSAS/MISSOURI MEDICARE HEALTH PLAN COMPARISONS (cont.)

	Healthpartners PARTNERS FOR SENIORS (H9005 - 004) Minneapolis/St. Paul	**Healthpartners** PARTNERS FOR SENIORS BASIC (H9005 - 002) Minneapolis/St. Paul	**Medica** (H2450 - 999) Minnesota	**Medica Health Plans** Basic (H9006 - 001) Minneapolis/St. Paul	**Medica Health Plans** Complete (H9006 - 003) Minneapolis/St. Paul
Premium (Part B - $45.50/month in 2000)	You pay $94.75 a month if you have Medicare Parts A and B.	You pay $94.75 a month if you have Medicare Parts A and B.		You pay $63.95 a month if you have Medicare Parts A and B.	You pay $279.95 a month if you have Medicare Parts A and B.
Physician Visits	You pay $10 for each visit with your personal physician.	You pay $15 for each visit with your personal physician.		You pay $15 for each visit with your personal physician.	You pay $5 for each visit with your personal physician.

	Healthpartners PARTNERS FOR SENIORS (H9005 - 004) Minneapolis/St. Paul	**Healthpartners** PARTNERS FOR SENIORS BASIC (H9005 - 002) Minneapolis/St. Paul	**Medica** (H2450 - 999) Minnesota	**Medica Health Plans** Basic (H9006 - 001) Minneapolis/St. Paul	**Medica Health Plans** Complete (H9006 - 003) Minneapolis/St. Paul
Inpatient Hospital	You pay nothing for your hospital stay. You are covered for additional days in the hospital. Contact plan for details.	You pay $100 for each admission to a plan hospital. You are covered for additional days in the hospital. Contact plan for details.		You pay $100 for each admission to a plan hospital. You are covered for additional days in the hospital. Contact plan for details.	You pay nothing for your hospital stay. You are covered for additional days in the hospital. Contact plan for details.
Doctor Choice	You need a referral to see a specialist some of the time. Contact plan for details.	You need a referral to see a specialist some of the time. Contact plan for details.		You need a referral to see a specialist, except for your annual GYN visit.	You need a referral to see a specialist, except for your annual GYN visit.

	Healthpartners PARTNERS FOR SENIORS (H9005 - 004) Minneapolis/St. Paul	**Healthpartners** PARTNERS FOR SENIORS (H9005 - 004) Minneapolis/St. Paul	**Healthpartners** PARTNERS FOR SENIORS BASIC (H9005 - 002) Minneapolis/St. Paul	**Medica** (H2450 - 999) Minneapolis/St. Paul	**Medica Health Plans** Basic (H9006 - 001) Minneapolis/St. Paul
Prescription Drugs	Prescription drugs are covered with an additional monthly premium of $175.25. You pay 20% per generic prescription. You pay 20% per brand name prescription. You have an unlimited prescription drug benefit. You must use plan-approved prescription drugs.	You pay 100% for most prescription drugs.		You pay 100% for most prescription drugs.	Prescription drugs are covered with limits. You pay 20% per generic prescription. You pay 20% per brand name prescription. You have an unlimited prescription drug benefit. You must use plan-approved prescription drugs. There are other limits on prescription drugs. Contact plan for details.
Physical Exams	You pay nothing for a physical exam. You are covered for an unlimited number of physical exams per year.	You pay nothing for a physical exam. You are covered for an unlimited number of physical exams per year.		You pay nothing for a physical exam. You are covered for 1 physical exam(s) per year.	You pay nothing for a physical exam. You are covered for 1 physical exam(s) per year.

	Healthpartners PARTNERS FOR SENIORS (H9005 - 004) Minneapolis/St. Paul	**Healthpartners** PARTNERS FOR SENIORS (H9005 - 004) Minneapolis/St. Paul	**Healthpartners** PARTNERS FOR SENIORS BASIC (H9005 - 002) Minneapolis/St. Paul	**Medica** (H2450 - 999) Minneapolis/St. Paul	**Medica Health Plans** Basic (H9006 - 001) Minneapolis/St. Paul
Vision Services	You have some coverage for routine eye exams. Contact plan for details.	You have some coverage for routine eye exams. Contact plan for details.		You have some coverage for routine eye exams. Contact plan for details.	You have some coverage for routine eye exams. Contact plan for details.
Dental	You are covered for 2 preventive dental exam(s) every 1 year(s). You pay $10 per preventive dental exam. You are covered for some other dental care beyond the basic Medicare benefit. Contact plan for details.	In general, you pay 100% for dental services.		In general, you pay 100% for dental services.	You are covered for 2 preventive dental exam(s) every 1 year(s). You pay $5 per preventive dental exam. You are covered for some other dental care beyond the basic Medicare benefit. Contact plan for details.

MINNESOTA/SOUTH DAKOTA/NEBRASKA/KANSAS/MISSOURI MEDICARE HEALTH PLAN COMPARISONS (cont.)

	Medica Health Plans Plus (H9006 - 002) Minneapolis/St. Paul	**Sioux Valley Health Plan of Minnesota** Basic Plan (H2403 - 002) Southwest Minnesota	**Sioux Valley Health Plan of Minnesota** Plus Plan (H2403 - 003) Southwest Minnesota	**Coventry Health Care Of KC, Inc** Advantra-Basic (H2672 - 001) Kansas and Missouri	**Good Health HMO, Inc.** Blue-Advantage 65 Basic Plan (H2656 - 001) Minnesota
Premium (Part B - $45.50/month in 2000)	You pay $74.95 a month if you have Medicare Parts A and B.	You pay $49 a month if you have Medicare Parts A and B.	You pay $99 a month if you have Medicare Parts A and B.	You pay nothing if you have Medicare Parts A and B.	You pay nothing if you have Medicare Parts A and B.
Physician Visits	You pay $5 for each visit with your personal physician.	You pay $10 for each visit with your personal physician.	You pay $10 for each visit with your personal physician.	You pay $10 for each visit with your personal physician.	You pay $10 for each visit with your personal physician.
Inpatient Hospital	You pay nothing for your hospital stay. You are covered for additional days in the hospital. Contact plan for details.	You pay nothing for your hospital stay. You are covered for additional days in the hospital. Contact plan for details.	You pay nothing for your hospital stay. You are covered for additional days in the hospital. Contact plan for details.	You pay nothing for your hospital stay. You are covered for additional days in the hospital. Contact plan for details.	You pay nothing for your hospital stay. You are covered for additional days in the hospital. Contact plan for details.
Doctor Choice	You need a referral to see a specialist, except for your annual GYN visit.	You do not need a referral to see a specialist.	You do not need a referral to see a specialist.	You need a referral to see a specialist, except for your annual GYN visit.	You need a referral to see a specialist, except for your annual GYN visit.

	Medica Health Plans Plus (H9006 - 002) Minneapolis/St. Paul	**Sioux Valley Health Plan of Minnesota** Basic Plan (H2403 - 002) Southwest Minnesota	**Sioux Valley Health Plan of Minnesota** Plus Plan (H2403 - 003) Southwest Minnesota	**Coventry Health Care Of KC, Inc** Advantra-Basic (H2672 - 001) Kansas and Missouri	**Good Health HMO, Inc.** Blue-Advantage 65 Basic Plan (H2656 - 001) Minnesota
Prescription Drugs	You pay 100% for most prescription drugs.	You pay 100% for most prescription drugs.	Prescription drugs are covered with limits. You pay $10 per generic prescription. You pay $20 per brand name prescription. Your generic and brand name prescription drugs are covered up to $1,000 per year. There is a monthly limit for prescription drugs. Contact plan for details.	Prescription drugs are covered with limits. You pay $10 per generic prescription. You pay $20 per brand name prescription. Your generic and brand name prescription drugs are covered up to $800 per year. If you do not use plan-approved drugs, your costs may be different.	Prescription drugs are covered with limits. You pay $10 per generic prescription. You pay $20 per brand name prescription. Your generic and brand name prescription drugs are covered up to $750 per year. You must use plan-approved prescription drugs. There is a quarterly limit for prescription drugs. Contact plan for details.
Physical Exams	You pay nothing for a physical exam. You are covered for 1 physical exam(s) per year.	You pay nothing for a physical exam. You are covered for 1 physical exam(s) per year.	You pay nothing for a physical exam. You are covered for 1 physical exam(s) per year.	You pay $10 for a physical exam. You are covered for 1 physical exam(s) per year.	You pay $10 for a physical exam. You are covered for an unlimited number of physical exams per year.

	Medica Health Plans Plus (H9006 - 002) Minneapolis/St. Paul	**Sioux Valley Health Plan of Minnesota** Basic Plan (H2403 - 002) Southwest Minnesota	**Sioux Valley Health Plan of Minnesota** Plus Plan (H2403 - 003) Southwest Minnesota	**Coventry Health Care Of KC, Inc** Advantra-Basic (H2672 - 001) Kansas and Missouri	**Good Health HMO, Inc.** Blue-Advantage 65 Basic Plan (H2656 - 001) Minnesota
Vision Services	You have some coverage for routine eye exams. Contact plan for details.	You have some coverage for glasses, contacts and routine eye exams. Contact plan for details.	You have some coverage for glasses, contacts and routine eye exams. Contact plan for details.	You have some coverage for glasses, contacts and routine eye exams. Contact plan for details.	You have some coverage for routine eye exams. Contact plan for details.
Dental	You are covered for 2 preventive dental exam(s) every 1 year(s). You pay $5 per preventive dental exam. You are covered for some other dental care beyond the basic Medicare benefit. Contact plan for details.	In general, you pay 100% for dental services.	In general, you pay 100% for dental services.	In general, you pay 100% for dental services.	In general, you pay 100% for dental services.

MINNESOTA/SOUTH DAKOTA/NEBRASKA/KANSAS/MISSOURI MEDICARE HEALTH PLAN COMPARISONS (cont.)

	Good Health HMO, Inc. Blue-Advantage 65 Bonus Plan (H2656 - 002) Missouri	**Good Health HMO, Inc.** Blue-Advantage 65 Regular Plan (H2656 - 003) Missouri	**Group Health Plan, Inc.** Advantra (H2663 - 001) St. Louis	**Group Health Plan, Inc.** Advantra (H2663 - 002) St. Louis and Central Missouri	**HealthNet** HealthNet Senior Excel Premier Plan (H2666 - 005) Kansas City
Premium (Part B - $45.50/month in 2000)	You pay $45 a month if you have Medicare Parts A and B.	You pay $59 a month if you have Medicare Parts A and B.	You pay nothing if you have Medicare Parts A and B.	You pay $35 a month if you have Medicare Parts A and B.	You pay $49 a month if you have Medicare Parts A and B.
Physician Visits	You pay $5 for each visit with your personal physician.	You pay $5 for each visit with your personal physician.	You pay $5 for each visit with your personal physician.	You pay $5 for each visit with your personal physician.	You pay $10 for each visit with your personal physician.
Inpatient Hospital	You pay nothing for your hospital stay. You are covered for additional days in the hospital. Contact plan for details.	You pay nothing for your hospital stay. You are covered for additional days in the hospital. Contact plan for details.	You pay $100 for each admission to a plan hospital. You are covered for additional days in the hospital. Contact plan for details.	You pay $100 for each admission to a plan hospital. You are covered for additional days in the hospital. Contact plan for details.	You pay $200 for each admission to a plan hospital. You are covered for additional days in the hospital. Contact plan for details.
Doctor Choice	You need a referral to see a specialist, except for your annual GYN visit.	You need a referral to see a specialist, except for your annual GYN visit.	You need a referral to see a specialist some of the time. Contact plan for details.	You need a referral to see a specialist some of the time. Contact plan for details.	You need a referral to see a specialist, except for your annual GYN visit.

	Good Health HMO, Inc. Blue-Advantage 65 Bonus Plan (H2656 - 002) Missouri	**Good Health HMO, Inc.** Blue-Advantage 65 Regular Plan (H2656 - 003) Missouri	**Group Health Plan, Inc.** Advantra (H2663 - 001) St. Louis	**Group Health Plan, Inc.** Advantra (H2663 - 002) St. Louis and Central Missouri	**HealthNet** HealthNet Senior Excel Premier Plan (H2666 - 005) Kansas City
Prescription Drugs	Prescription drugs are covered with limits. You pay $7 per generic prescription. You pay $7 per brand name prescription. You have an unlimited generic drug benefit. Your brand name prescription drugs are covered up to $100 per year. There are other limits on prescription drugs. Contact plan for details.	Prescription drugs are covered with limits. You pay $5 per generic prescription. You pay $5 per brand name prescription. Your generic and brand name prescription drugs are covered up to $450 per year.	Prescription drugs are covered with limits. You pay $10 per generic prescription. You pay $20 per brand name prescription. You have an unlimited generic drug benefit. Your brand name prescription drugs are covered up to $500 per year. Contact plan for details on how this limit applies. If you do not use plan-approved drugs, your costs may be different. There are other limits on prescription drugs. Contact plan for details.	Prescription drugs are covered with limits. You pay $10 per generic prescription. You pay $20 per brand name prescription. You have an unlimited generic drug benefit. Your brand name prescription drugs are covered up to $500 per year. Contact plan for details on how this limit applies. If you do not use plan-approved drugs, your costs may be different. There are other limits on prescription drugs. Contact plan for details.	Prescription drugs are covered with limits. You pay $10 per generic prescription. You pay $40 per brand name prescription. You have an unlimited generic drug benefit. Your brand name prescription drugs are covered up to $700 per year. Contact plan for details on how this limit applies. If you do not use plan-approved drugs, your costs may be different.
Physical Exams	You pay $5 for a physical exam. You are covered for an unlimited number of physical exams per year.	You pay $5 for a physical exam. You are covered for an unlimited number of physical exams per year.	You pay $5 for a physical exam. You are covered for 1 physical exam(s) per year.	You pay $5 for a physical exam. You are covered for 1 physical exam(s) per year.	You pay $10 for a physical exam. You are covered for 1 physical exam(s) per year.

	Good Health HMO, Inc. Blue-Advantage 65 Bonus Plan (H2656 - 002) Missouri	**Good Health HMO, Inc.** Blue-Advantage 65 Regular Plan (H2656 - 003) Missouri	**Group Health Plan, Inc.** Advantra (H2663 – 001) St. Louis	**Group Health Plan, Inc.** Advantra (H2663 - 002) St. Louis and Central Missouri	**HealthNet** HealthNet Senior Excel Premier Plan (H2666 - 005) Kansas City
Vision Services	You have some coverage for glasses and routine eye exams. Contact plan for details.	You have some coverage for glasses and routine eye exams. Contact plan for details.	You have some coverage for glasses and routine eye exams. Contact plan for details.	You have some coverage for glasses and routine eye exams. Contact plan for details.	You have some coverage for glasses, contacts and routine eye exams. Contact plan for details.
Dental	You are covered for 2 preventive dental exam(s) every 1 year(s). You pay nothing per preventive dental exam.	You are covered for 2 preventive dental exam(s) every 1 year(s). You pay nothing per preventive dental exam.	You are covered for 1 preventive dental exam(s) every 1 year(s). You pay nothing per preventive dental exam. You are covered for some other dental care beyond the basic Medicare benefit. Contact plan for details.	You are covered for 1 preventive dental exam(s) every 1 year(s). You pay nothing per preventive dental exam. You are covered for some other dental care beyond the basic Medicare benefit. Contact plan for details.	In general, you pay 100% for dental services.

MINNESOTA/SOUTH DAKOTA/NEBRASKA/KANSAS/MISSOURI MEDICARE HEALTH PLAN COMPARISONS (cont.)

	HealthNet HealthNet Senior Excel Standard Plan (H2666 - 004) Kansas City area	**HMO Missouri, Inc.** Blue Horizons Medicare HMO (H2659 - 001) St. Louis	**Humana Kansas City, Inc.** Humana Gold Plus - Kansas City Premium (H2649 - 005) Kansas City	**Humana Kansas City, Inc.** Humana Gold Plus - Kansas City Value (H2649 - 004) Kansas City	**Kaiser Foundation Hp of KS City, Inc.** Senior Advantage Gold (H1751 - 003) Kansas City
Premium (Part B - $45.50/month in 2000)	You pay nothing if you have Medicare Parts A and B.	You pay nothing if you have Medicare Parts A and B.	You pay $130 a month if you have Medicare Parts A and B.	You pay $10 a month if you have Medicare Parts A and B.	You pay $39 a month if you have Medicare Parts A and B.
Physician Visits	You pay $15 for each visit with your personal physician.	You pay $10 for each visit with your personal physician.	You pay $7 for each visit with your personal physician.	You pay $12 for each visit with your personal physician.	You pay $5 for each visit with your personal physician.
Inpatient Hospital	You pay $200 for each admission to a plan hospital. You are covered for additional days in the hospital. Contact plan for details.	You pay nothing for your hospital stay. You are covered for additional days in the hospital. Contact plan for details.	You pay nothing for your hospital stay. You are covered for additional days in the hospital. Contact plan for details.	You pay nothing for your hospital stay. You are covered for additional days in the hospital. Contact plan for details.	You pay nothing for your hospital stay. You are covered for additional days in the hospital. Contact plan for details.
Doctor Choice	You need a referral to see a specialist, except for your annual GYN visit.	You need a referral to see a specialist some of the time. Contact plan for details.	You need a referral to see a specialist some of the time. Contact plan for details.	You need a referral to see a specialist some of the time. Contact plan for details.	You need a referral to see a specialist some of the time. Contact plan for details.

	HealthNet HealthNet Senior Excel Standard Plan (H2666 - 004) Kansas City area	**HMO Missouri, Inc.** Blue Horizons Medicare HMO (H2659 - 001) St. Louis	**Humana Kansas City, Inc.** Humana Gold Plus - Kansas City Premium (H2649 - 005) Kansas City	**Humana Kansas City, Inc.** Humana Gold Plus - Kansas City Value (H2649 - 004) Kansas City	**Kaiser Foundation Hp of KS City, Inc.** Senior Advantage Gold (H1751 - 003) Kansas City
Prescription Drugs	Prescription drugs are covered with limits. You pay $10 per generic prescription. You have an unlimited generic drug benefit. If you do not use plan-approved drugs, your costs may be different.	Prescription drugs are covered with limits. You pay $5 per generic prescription. You pay $12 per brand name prescription. Your prescription drugs are covered up to $500 per year. Contact plan for details on how this limit applies. If you do not use plan-approved drugs, your costs may be different. There is a monthly and other limits on prescription drugs. Contact plan for details.	Prescription drugs are covered with limits. You pay $5 per generic prescription. You pay $15 per brand name prescription. You have an unlimited generic drug benefit. Your brand name prescription drugs are covered up to $1,200 per year. If you do not use plan-approved drugs, your costs may be different. There is a quarterly limit for prescription drugs. Contact plan for details.	Prescription drugs are covered with limits. You pay $5 per generic prescription. You pay $20 per brand name prescription. You have an unlimited generic drug benefit. Your brand name prescription drugs are covered up to $750 per year. If you do not use plan-approved drugs, your costs may be different. There is a quarterly limit for prescription drugs. Contact plan for details.	Prescription drugs are covered with limits. You pay $10 per generic prescription. You pay $20 per brand name prescription. You have an unlimited generic drug benefit. Your brand name prescription drugs are covered up to $1,200 per year. You must use plan-approved prescription drugs.
Physical Exams	You pay $15 for a physical exam. You are covered for 1 physical exam(s) per year.	You pay $10 for a physical exam. You are covered for an unlimited number of physical exams per year.	You pay nothing for a physical exam. You are covered for 1 physical exam(s) per year.	You pay nothing for a physical exam. You are covered for 1 physical exam(s) per year.	You pay nothing for a physical exam. You are covered for 1 physical exam(s) per year.

	HealthNet HealthNet Senior Excel Standard Plan (H2666 - 004) Kansas City area	**HMO Missouri, Inc.** Blue Horizons Medicare HMO (H2659 - 001) St. Louis	**Humana Kansas City, Inc.** Humana Gold Plus - Kansas City Premium (H2649 - 005) Kansas City	**Humana Kansas City, Inc.** Humana Gold Plus - Kansas City Value (H2649 - 004) Kansas City	**Kaiser Foundation Hp of KS City, Inc.** Senior Advantage Gold (H1751 - 003) Kansas City
Vision Services	You have some coverage for routine eye exams. Contact plan for details.	Routine eye exams and glasses are not covered. You are covered for diagnostic and therapeutic services for the eye.	You have some coverage for glasses and routine eye exams. Contact plan for details.	You have some coverage for glasses and routine eye exams. Contact plan for details.	You have some coverage for glasses, contacts and routine eye exams. Contact plan for details.
Dental	In general, you pay 100% for dental services.	In general, you pay 100% for dental services.	You are covered for some other dental care beyond the basic Medicare benefit. Contact plan for details.	You are covered for some other dental care beyond the basic Medicare benefit. Contact plan for details.	You are covered for 2 preventive dental exam(s) every 1 year(s). You pay $5 per preventive dental exam. You are covered for some other dental care beyond the basic Medicare benefit. Contact plan for details.

MINNESOTA/SOUTH DAKOTA/NEBRASKA/KANSAS/MISSOURI MEDICARE HEALTH PLAN COMPARISONS (cont.)

	Kaiser Foundation Hp of KS City, Inc. Senior Advantage Silver (H1751 - 002) Kansas City	**Mercy Health Plans, Inc.** PremierPlus (H2668 - 002) St. Louis	**Mercy Health Plans, Inc.** PremierPlus (H2668 - 003) St. Louis	**Total Health Care** Total Health Care-65 (H2652 - 001) Missouri	**United Healthcare of the Midwest, Inc.** Medicare Complete--St. Louis (H2654 - 003)
Premium (Part B - $45.50/month in 2000)	You pay nothing if you have Medicare Parts A and B.	You pay $39 a month if you have Medicare Parts A and B.	You pay $69 a month if you have Medicare Parts A and B.	You pay $110 a month if you have Medicare Parts A and B.	You pay nothing if you have Medicare Parts A and B.
Physician Visits	You pay $10 for each visit with your personal physician.	You pay $10 for each visit with your personal physician.	You pay $10 for each visit with your personal physician.	You pay $5 for each visit with your personal physician.	You pay $10 for each visit with your personal physician.
Inpatient Hospital	You pay nothing for your hospital stay. You are covered for additional days in the hospital. Contact plan for details.	You pay nothing for your hospital stay. You are covered for additional days in the hospital. Contact plan for details.	You pay nothing for your hospital stay. You are covered for additional days in the hospital. Contact plan for details.	You pay nothing for your hospital stay. You are covered for additional days in the hospital. Contact plan for details.	You are covered for additional days in the hospital. Contact plan for details.
Doctor Choice	You need a referral to see a specialist some of the time. Contact plan for details.	You need a referral to see a specialist, except for your annual GYN visit.	You need a referral to see a specialist, except for your annual GYN visit.	You need a referral to see a specialist, except for your annual GYN visit.	You need a referral to see a specialist some of the time. Contact plan for details.

	Kaiser Foundation Hp of KS City, Inc. Senior Advantage Silver (H1751 - 002) Kansas City	**Mercy Health Plans, Inc.** PremierPlus (H2668 - 002) St. Louis	**Mercy Health Plans, Inc.** PremierPlus (H2668 - 003) St. Louis	**Total Health Care** Total Health Care-65 (H2652 - 001) Missouri	**United Healthcare of the Midwest, Inc.** Medicare Complete--St. Louis (H2654 - 003)
Prescription Drugs	Prescription drugs are covered with limits. You pay $10 per generic prescription. You pay $20 per brand name prescription. You have an unlimited generic drug benefit. Your brand name prescription drugs are covered up to $750 per year. You must use plan-approved prescription drugs.	Prescription drugs are covered with limits. You pay $10 per generic prescription. You pay $10 per brand name prescription. Your generic and brand name prescription drugs are covered up to $500 per year. You must use plan-approved prescription drugs.	Prescription drugs are covered with limits. You pay $10 per generic prescription. You pay $10 per brand name prescription. You have an unlimited generic drug benefit. Your brand name prescription drugs are covered up to $500 per year. You must use plan-approved prescription drugs.	Prescription drugs are covered with limits. You pay 50% per generic prescription. You pay 50% per brand name prescription. Your generic and brand name prescription drugs are covered up to $250 per year. There are other limits on prescription drugs. Contact plan for details.	Prescription drugs are covered with limits. You pay $5 per generic prescription. You pay $35 per brand name prescription. Your generic and brand name prescription drugs are covered up to $500 per year. You must use plan-approved prescription drugs. There are other limits on prescription drugs. Contact plan for details.
Physical Exams	You pay nothing for a physical exam.	You pay $10 for a physical exam. You are covered for 1 physical exam(s) per year.	You pay $10 for a physical exam. You are covered for 1 physical exam(s) per year.	You pay $5 for a physical exam.	You pay $10 for a physical exam. You are covered for 1 physical exam(s) per year.
Vision Services	You have some coverage for glasses, contacts and routine eye exams. Contact plan for details.	You have some coverage for routine eye exams. Contact plan for details.	You have some coverage for glasses and routine eye exams. Contact plan for details.	You have some coverage for routine eye exams. Contact plan for details.	You have some coverage for glasses, contacts and routine eye exams. Contact plan for details.

	Kaiser Foundation Hp of KS City, Inc. Senior Advantage Silver (H1751 - 002) Kansas City	**Mercy Health Plans, Inc.** PremierPlus (H2668 - 002) St. Louis	**Mercy Health Plans, Inc.** PremierPlus (H2668 - 003) St. Louis	**Total Health Care** Total Health Care-65 (H2652 - 001) Missouri	**United Healthcare of the Midwest, Inc.** Medicare Complete--St. Louis (H2654 - 003)
Dental	You are covered for 2 preventive dental exam(s) every 1 year(s). You pay $15 per preventive dental exam. You are covered for some other dental care beyond the basic Medicare benefit. Contact plan for details.	In general, you pay 100% for dental services.	You are covered for 2 preventive dental exam(s) every 1 year(s). You pay $10 per preventive dental exam. You are covered for some other dental care beyond the basic Medicare benefit. Contact plan for details.	In general, you pay 100% for dental services.	In general, you pay 100% for dental services.

IOWA/MINNESOTA/MISSOURI/KANSAS/NEBRASKA/SOUTH DAKOTA MEDICARE QUALITY RATINGS

	Satisfaction Indicators			
Plan Name	Overall Rating of Managed Care Plan	Overall Rating of Health Care Patients Received	Doctors Who Communicate Well	Ease of Getting Referrals to a Specialist
First Plan of Minnesota	Data not available	Data not available	Data not available	Data not available
Healthpartners	Data not available	Data not available	Data not available	Data not available
Healthpartners	39%	45%	65%	86%
Medica	Data not available	Data not available	Data not available	Data not available
Medica Health Plans	47%	48%	65%	91%
Sioux Valley Health Plan of Minnesota	Data not available	Data not available	Data not available	Data not available
Coventry Health Care Of Iowa, Inc.	Data not available	Data not available	Data not available	Data not available
John Deere Health Plan, Inc.	Data not available	Data not available	Data not available	Data not available
Medical Associates Health Plan, Inc.	43%	52%	68%	88%
Sioux Valley Health Plan	Data not available	Data not available	Data not available	Data not available
United Healthcare of the Midlands, Inc.	60%	53%	73%	90%
Coventry Health Care Of KC, Inc	Data not available	Data not available	Data not available	Data not available
Good Health HMO, Inc.	48%	54%	71%	87%
Group Health Plan, Inc.	55%	52%	71%	84%
HealthNet	55%	56%	72%	88%

HMO Missouri, Inc.	43%	54%	72%	86%
Humana Kansas City, Inc.	46%	50%	68%	81%
Kaiser Foundation Hp of KS City, Inc.	42%	47%	68%	86%
Mercy Health Plans, Inc.	Data not available	Data not available	Data not available	Data not available
Mercy Health Plans, Inc.	Data not available	Data not available	Data not available	Data not available
Total Health Care	58%	58%	71%	95%
United Healthcare of the Midwest, Inc.	53%	53%	72%	82%

APPENDIX D

COFFEE, GEORGIA

(includes parts of Florida, Georgia, and South Carolina)

1) **Map of Demonstration Area**
2) **Summary of Local FEHBP Options**
3) **Summary of Medicare+Choice Options**

FEHBP Demonstration, Coffee, Georgia

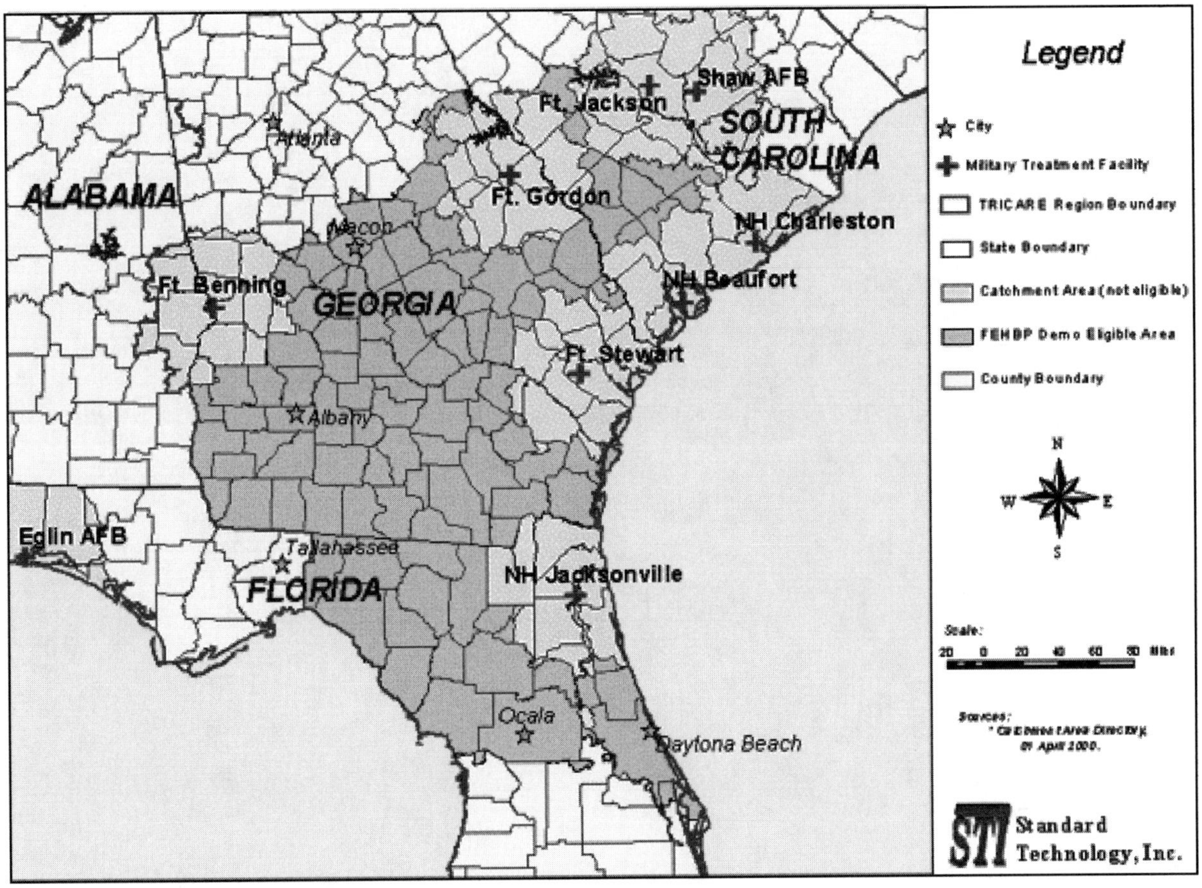

Coffee, Georgia FEHBP Options

			Primary care doctor	Hospital room copay/ insurance	Prescription drugs, generic	Prescription drugs, brand	Primary care doctor office copay	Hospital inpatient R&B charges	Prescription drugs, generic	R/Brand/ Local
			In Network You Pay				Out of Network You Pay			
Blue Cross and Blue Shield -Std	POS	Athens/Atl/Augusta/Col/ Macon/Savannah	$10	0	$5	$15	25%	30%	45%	45%
							Your share of premium Monthly			
							Self only		Self & family	
							65.09		144.69	

Coffee, Georgia FEHBP Quality Ratings

	Satisfaction Indicators 1=above average, 2=average, 3=below average							
Plan Name	Overall plan satisfaction	Getting needed care	Getting care quickly	How well doctors communicate	Courteous and helpful office staff	Customer service	Claims processing	Child survey Overall satisfactoin
Free State Health Plan	2	3	3	2	2	2	1	2

GEORGIA MEDICARE HEALTH PLAN COMPARISONS

	Kaiser Foundation Health Plan of GA, Inc. Kaiser Permanente Senior Advantage (H1170 - 002)Georgia	**United HealthCare Insurance Company** EverCare (H1151 - 001) Georgia	**Aetna U.S. Healthcare** Medicare 10 (H1015 - 003) Florida	**Aetna U.S. Healthcare** Medicare 10 Base (H1015 - 002) Florida	**Aetna U.S. Healthcare** Medicare 5 (H1015 - 004) Florida
Premium (Part B - $45.50/month in 2000)	You pay nothing if you have Medicare Parts A and B.	You pay nothing if you have Medicare Parts A and B.	You pay $83 a month if you have Medicare Parts A and B.	You pay $25 a month if you have Medicare Parts A and B.	You pay $118 a month if you have Medicare Parts A and B.
Physician Visits	You pay $10 for each visit with your personal physician.	You pay nothing to see your personal physician.	You pay $10 for each visit with your personal physician.	You pay $10 for each visit with your personal physician.	You pay $5 for each visit with your personal physician.
Inpatient Hospital	You pay nothing for your hospital stay. You are covered for additional days in the hospital. Contact plan for details.	You pay nothing for your hospital stay. You are covered for additional days in the hospital. Contact plan for details.	You pay nothing for your hospital stay. You are covered for additional days in the hospital. Contact plan for details.	You pay nothing for your hospital stay. You are covered for additional days in the hospital. Contact plan for details.	You pay nothing for your hospital stay. You are covered for additional days in the hospital. Contact plan for details.
Doctor Choice	You need a referral to see a specialist some of the time. Contact plan for details.	You need a referral to see a specialist some of the time. Contact plan for details.	You need a referral to see a specialist some of the time. Contact plan for details.	You need a referral to see a specialist some of the time. Contact plan for details.	You need a referral to see a specialist some of the time. Contact plan for details.

	Kaiser Foundation Health Plan of GA, Inc. Kaiser Permanente Senior Advantage (H1170 - 002) Georgia	**United HealthCare Insurance Company** EverCare (H1151 - 001) Georgia	**Aetna U.S. Healthcare** Medicare 10 (H1015 - 003) Florida	**Aetna U.S. Healthcare** Medicare 10 Base (H1015 - 002) Florida	**Aetna U.S. Healthcare** Medicare 5 (H1015 - 004) Florida
Prescription Drugs	Prescription drugs are covered with limits. You pay $15 per generic prescription. You pay $15 per brand name prescription. Your prescription drugs are covered up to $500 per year. Contact plan for details on how this limit applies. You must use plan-approved prescription drugs.	You pay 100% for most prescription drugs.	Prescription drugs are covered with limits. You pay $15 per generic prescription. You pay $20 per brand name prescription. You have an unlimited generic drug benefit. Your brand name prescription drugs are covered up to $500 per year. If you do not use plan-approved drugs, your costs may be different. There are other limits on prescription drugs. Contact plan for details.	Prescription drugs are covered with limits. There are other limits on prescription drugs. Contact plan for details.	Prescription drugs are covered with limits. You pay $15 per generic prescription. You pay $20 per brand name prescription. You have an unlimited generic drug benefit. Your brand name prescription drugs are covered up to $1,000 per year. If you do not use plan-approved drugs, your costs may be different. There are other limits on prescription drugs. Contact plan for details.

	Kaiser Foundation Health Plan of GA, Inc. Kaiser Permanente Senior Advantage (H1170 - 002) Georgia	**United HealthCare Insurance Company** EverCare (H1151 - 001) Georgia	**Aetna U.S. Healthcare** Medicare 10 (H1015 - 003) Florida	**Aetna U.S. Healthcare** Medicare 10 Base (H1015 - 002) Florida	**Aetna U.S. Healthcare** Medicare 5 (H1015 - 004) Florida
Physical Exams	You pay $10 for a physical exam. You are covered for an unlimited number of physical exams per year.	You pay nothing for a physical exam. You are covered for an unlimited number of physical exams per year.	You pay $10 for a physical exam. You are covered for 1 physical exam(s) per year.	You pay $10 for a physical exam. You are covered for 1 physical exam(s) per year.	You pay $5 for a physical exam. You are covered for 1 physical exam(s) per year.
Vision Services	You have some coverage for glasses, contacts and routine eye exams. Contact plan for details.	Routine eye exams and glasses are not covered. You are covered for diagnostic and therapeutic services for the eye.	You have some coverage for glasses, contacts and routine eye exams. Contact plan for details.	You have some coverage for glasses, contacts and routine eye exams. Contact plan for details.	You have some coverage for glasses, contacts and routine eye exams. Contact plan for details.
Dental	In general, you pay 100% for dental services.	In general, you pay 100% for dental services.	You are covered for some other dental care beyond the basic Medicare benefit. Contact plan for details.	You are covered for some other dental care beyond the basic Medicare benefit. Contact plan for details.	You are covered for 2 preventive dental exam(s) every 1 year(s). You pay $5 per preventive dental exam. You are covered for some other dental care beyond the basic Medicare benefit. Contact plan for details.

GEORGIA MEDICARE HEALTH PLAN COMPARISONS (cont.)

	AvMed, Inc. Avmed Health Plan (H1061 - 001) Orange and Oceola	**Capital Group Health Svc Of FL** Capital Health Plan Medicare Gold Plan (H1010 - 001) Tallahassee area	**Capital Group Health Svc Of FL** CAPITAL HEALTH PLAN MEDICARE LOW OPTION (H1010 - 002) Tallahassee area	**CIGNA HealthCare of Florida, Inc.** CIGNA HealthCare for Seniors $0 Individual (H1098 - 001) Orange and Osceola	**Health Options, Inc.\BC and BS of FL** Medicare & More (H1095 - 001) Orange and Osceola
Premium (Part B - $45.50/month in 2000)	You pay $109 a month if you have Medicare Parts A and B.	You pay $125.80 a month if you have Medicare Parts A and B.	You pay $79.90 a month if you have Medicare Parts A and B.	You pay nothing if you have Medicare Parts A and B.	You pay $40 a month if you have Medicare Parts A and B.
Physician Visits	You pay $10 for each visit with your personal physician.	You pay $5 for each visit with your personal physician.	You pay $5 for each visit with your personal physician.	You pay $10 for each visit with your personal physician.	You pay $10 for each visit with your personal physician.
Inpatient Hospital	You are covered for additional days in the hospital. Contact plan for details.	You pay nothing for your hospital stay.	You pay nothing for your hospital stay.	You pay nothing for your hospital stay. You are covered for additional days in the hospital. Contact plan for details.	You pay $200 for each admission to a plan hospital. You are covered for additional days in the hospital. Contact plan for details.
Doctor Choice	You need a referral to see a specialist some of the time. Contact plan for details.	You need a referral to see a specialist some of the time. Contact plan for details.	You need a referral to see a specialist some of the time. Contact plan for details.	You need a referral to see a specialist some of the time. Contact plan for details.	You need a referral to see a specialist some of the time. Contact plan for details.

	AvMed, Inc. Avmed Health Plan (H1061 - 001) Orange and Oceola	**Capital Group Health Svc Of FL** Capital Health Plan Medicare Gold Plan (H1010 - 001) Tallahassee area	**Capital Group Health Svc Of FL** CAPITAL HEALTH PLAN MEDICARE LOW OPTION (H1010 - 002) Tallahassee area	**CIGNA HealthCare of Florida, Inc.** CIGNA HealthCare for Seniors $0 Individual (H1098 - 001) Orange and Osceola	**Health Options, Inc.\BC and BS of FL** Medicare & More (H1095 - 001) Orange and Osceola
Prescription Drugs	Prescription drugs are covered with limits. You pay $10 per generic prescription. You pay $20 per brand name prescription. Your generic and brand name prescription drugs are covered up to $600 per year. If you do not use plan-approved drugs, your costs may be different. There is a quarterly limit for prescription drugs. Contact plan for details.	Prescription drugs are covered with limits. You pay $7 per generic prescription. You pay $20 per brand name prescription. Your generic and brand name prescription drugs are covered up to $1,000 per year. If you do not use plan-approved drugs, your costs may be different. There are other limits on prescription drugs. Contact plan for details.	You pay 100% for most prescription drugs.	Prescription drugs are covered with limits. You pay $7 per generic prescription. You pay $15 per brand name prescription. You have an unlimited generic drug benefit. Your brand name prescription drugs are covered up to $1,000 per year. If you do not use plan-approved drugs, your costs may be different.	Prescription drugs are covered with limits. You pay $3 per generic prescription. You pay $15 per brand name prescription. You have an unlimited generic drug benefit. Your brand name prescription drugs are covered up to $1,000 per year. If you do not use plan-approved drugs, your costs may be different. There are other limits on prescription drugs. Contact plan for details.
Physical Exams	You pay $10 for a physical exam. You are covered for an unlimited number of physical exams per year.	You pay $5 for a physical exam. You are covered for an unlimited number of physical exams per year.	You pay $5 for a physical exam.	You pay $10 for a physical exam. You are covered for 1 physical exam(s) per year.	You pay $10 for a physical exam. You are covered for an unlimited number of physical exams per year.
Vision Services	You have some coverage for glasses, contacts and routine eye exams. Contact plan for details.	You have some coverage for routine eye exams. Contact plan for details.	Routine eye exams and glasses are not covered. You are covered for diagnostic and therapeutic services for the eye.	You have some coverage for glasses, contacts and routine eye exams. Contact plan for details.	You have some coverage for glasses, contacts and routine eye exams. Contact plan for details.

	AvMed, Inc. Avmed Health Plan (H1061 - 001) Orange and Oceola	**Capital Group Health Svc Of FL** Capital Health Plan Medicare Gold Plan (H1010 - 001) Tallahassee area	**Capital Group Health Svc Of FL** CAPITAL HEALTH PLAN MEDICARE LOW OPTION (H1010 - 002) Tallahassee area	**CIGNA HealthCare of Florida, Inc.** CIGNA HealthCare for Seniors $0 Individual (H1098 - 001) Orange and Osceola	**Health Options, Inc.\BC and BS of FL** Medicare & More (H1095 - 001) Orange and Osceola
Dental	In general, you pay 100% for dental services.	In general, you pay 100% for dental services.	In general, you pay 100% for dental services.	In general, you pay 100% for dental services.	In general, you pay 100% for dental services.

GEORGIA MEDICARE HEALTH PLAN COMPARISONS (cont.)

	Humana Medical Plan, Inc. Humana Gold Access - Daytona (H1036 - 015) Daytona	**Humana Medical Plan, Inc.** Humana Gold Plus - Daytona (H1036 - 016) Daytona	**Humana Medical Plan, Inc.** Humana Gold Plus - Jacksonville Value (H1036 - 012) Jacksonville	**Prudential HealthCare, Inc.** Prudential HealthCare SeniorCare (H1070 - 001) Jacksonville	**Well Care HMO, Inc.** Well Care Choice Medicare Plan (H1032 - 002) Florida
Premium (Part B - $45.50/month in 2000)	You pay $49 a month if you have Medicare Parts A and B.	You pay $10 a month if you have Medicare Parts A and B.	You pay $39 a month if you have Medicare Parts A and B.	You pay $50 a month if you have Medicare Parts A and B.	You pay nothing if you have Medicare Parts A and B.
Physician Visits	You pay $7 for each visit with your personal physician.	You pay $5 for each visit with your personal physician.	You pay $15 for each visit with your personal physician.	You pay $15 for each visit with your personal physician.	You pay $5 for each visit with your personal physician.
Inpatient Hospital	You pay $100 for each admission to a plan hospital. You are covered for additional days in the hospital. Contact plan for details.	You pay nothing for each admission to a plan hospital. You are covered for additional days in the hospital. Contact plan for details.	You pay $200 for each admission to a plan hospital. You are covered for additional days in the hospital. Contact plan for details.	You pay nothing for your hospital stay. You are covered for additional days in the hospital. Contact plan for details.	You pay nothing for your hospital stay. You are covered for additional days in the hospital. Contact plan for details.
Doctor Choice	You do not need a referral to see a specialist.	You need a referral to see a specialist some of the time. Contact plan for details.	You need a referral to see a specialist some of the time. Contact plan for details.	You need a referral to see a specialist some of the time. Contact plan for details.	You need a referral to see a specialist, except for your annual GYN visit.

	Humana Medical Plan, Inc. Humana Gold Access - Daytona (H1036 - 015)	**Humana Medical Plan, Inc.** Humana Gold Plus - Daytona (H1036 - 016)	**Humana Medical Plan, Inc.** Humana Gold Plus - Jacksonville Value (H1036 - 012)	**Prudential HealthCare, Inc.** Prudential HealthCare SeniorCare (H1070 - 001) Jacksonville	**Well Care HMO, Inc.** Well Care Choice Medicare Plan (H1032 - 002) Florida
Prescription Drugs	Prescription drugs are covered with limits. You pay $7 per generic prescription. You have an unlimited prescription drug benefit. There are other limits on prescription drugs. Contact plan for details.	Prescription drugs are covered with limits. You pay $5 per generic prescription. You pay $15 per brand name prescription. You have an unlimited generic drug benefit. Your brand name prescription drugs are covered up to $600 per year. If you do not use plan-approved drugs, your costs may be different. There is a monthly limit for prescription drugs. Contact plan for details.	Prescription drugs are covered with limits. You pay $5 per generic prescription. You pay $15 per brand name prescription. You have an unlimited generic drug benefit. Your brand name prescription drugs are covered up to $600 per year. Contact plan for details on how this limit applies. If you do not use plan-approved drugs, your costs may be different. There is a monthly limit for prescription drugs. Contact plan for details.	Prescription drugs are covered with limits. You pay $7 per generic prescription. You pay $20 per brand name prescription. Your generic and brand name prescription drugs are covered up to $500 per year. You must use plan-approved prescription drugs.	Prescription drugs are covered with limits. You pay $5 per generic prescription. You pay $15 per brand name prescription. You have an unlimited generic drug benefit. Your brand name prescription drugs are covered up to $1,500 per year. If you do not use plan-approved drugs, your costs may be different. There is a quarterly limit for prescription drugs. Contact plan for details.
Physical Exams	You pay nothing for a physical exam. You are covered for 1 physical exam(s) per year.	You pay nothing for a physical exam. You are covered for 1 physical exam(s) per year.	You pay nothing for a physical exam. You are covered for 1 physical exam(s) per year.	You pay $15 for a physical exam. You are covered for an unlimited number of physical exams per year.	You pay nothing for a physical exam. You are covered for 1 physical exam(s) per year.

	Humana Medical Plan, Inc. Humana Gold Access - Daytona (H1036 - 015)	**Humana Medical Plan, Inc.** Humana Gold Plus - Daytona (H1036 - 016)	**Humana Medical Plan, Inc.** Humana Gold Plus - Jacksonville Value (H1036 - 012)	**Prudential HealthCare, Inc.** Prudential HealthCare SeniorCare (H1070 - 001) Jacksonville	**Well Care HMO, Inc.** Well Care Choice Medicare Plan (H1032 - 002) Florida
Vision Services	You have some coverage for glasses, contacts and routine eye exams. Contact plan for details.	You have some coverage for glasses, contacts and routine eye exams. Contact plan for details.	You have some coverage for glasses, contacts and routine eye exams. Contact plan for details.	Routine eye exams and glasses are not covered. You are covered for diagnostic and therapeutic services for the eye.	You have some coverage for glasses and routine eye exams. Contact plan for details.
Dental	You are covered for some other dental care beyond the basic Medicare benefit. Contact plan for details.	You are covered for some other dental care beyond the basic Medicare benefit. Contact plan for details.	You are covered for some other dental care beyond the basic Medicare benefit. Contact plan for details.	In general, you pay 100% for dental services.	You are covered for 1 preventive dental exam(s) every 1 year(s). You pay nothing per preventive dental exam. You are covered for some other dental care beyond the basic Medicare benefit. Contact plan for details.

GEORGIA MEDICARE HEALTH PLAN COMPARISONS (cont.)

	Well Care HMO, Inc. Well Care Choice Medicare Plan (H1032 - 004) Florida
Premium (Part B - $45.50/month in 2000)	You pay nothing if you have Medicare Parts A and B.
Physician Visits	You pay $5 for each visit with your personal physician.
Inpatient Hospital	You pay nothing for your hospital stay. You are covered for additional days in the hospital. Contact plan for details.
Doctor Choice	You need a referral to see a specialist, except for your annual GYN visit.
Prescription Drugs	Prescription drugs are covered with limits. You pay $5 per generic prescription. You pay $15 per brand name prescription. You have an unlimited generic drug benefit. Your brand name prescription drugs are covered up to $1,500 per year. If you do not use plan-approved drugs, your costs may be different. There is a quarterly limit for prescription drugs. Contact plan for details.
Physical Exams	You pay nothing for a physical exam. You are covered for 1 physical exam(s) per year.
Vision Services	You have some coverage for glasses and routine eye exams. Contact plan for details.
Dental	You are covered for 1 preventive dental exam(s) every 1 year(s). You pay nothing per preventive dental exam. You are covered for some other dental care beyond the basic Medicare benefit. Contact plan for details.

GEORGIA MEDICARE QUALITY RATINGS

Plan Name	Satisfaction Indicators			
	Overall Rating of Managed Care Plan	Overall Rating of Health Care Patients Received	Doctors Who Communicate Well	Ease of Getting Referrals to a Specialist
Kaiser Foundation Health Plan of GA, Inc.	52%	55%	79%	90%
United HealthCare Insurance Company	Data not available	Data not available	Data not available	Data not available
United Healthcare of Georgia, Inc.	51%	52%	73%	84%
Aetna US Healthcare	Data not available	Data not available	Data not available	Data not available
AvMed, Inc.	54%	54%	72%	79%
Capital Group Hlth Svc Of FL	61%	50%	71%	92%
Cigna Healthcare of Florida, Inc.	48%	55%	71%	79%
Health Options, Inc.\BC and BS of FL	49%	52%	70%	80%
Humana Medical Plan, Inc./(Jacksonville)	41%	44%	65%	80%
Humana Medical Plan, Inc./(Tampa)	48%	48%	67%	82%
Prudential HealthCare, Inc.	54%	52%	71%	87%
Well Care HMO, Inc.	Data not available	Data not available	Data not available	Data not available

APPENDIX E

DALLAS, TEXAS

1) Map of Demonstration Area
2) Summary of Local FEHBP Options
3) Summary of Medicare+Choice Options

FEBHP Demonstration: Dallas, Texas

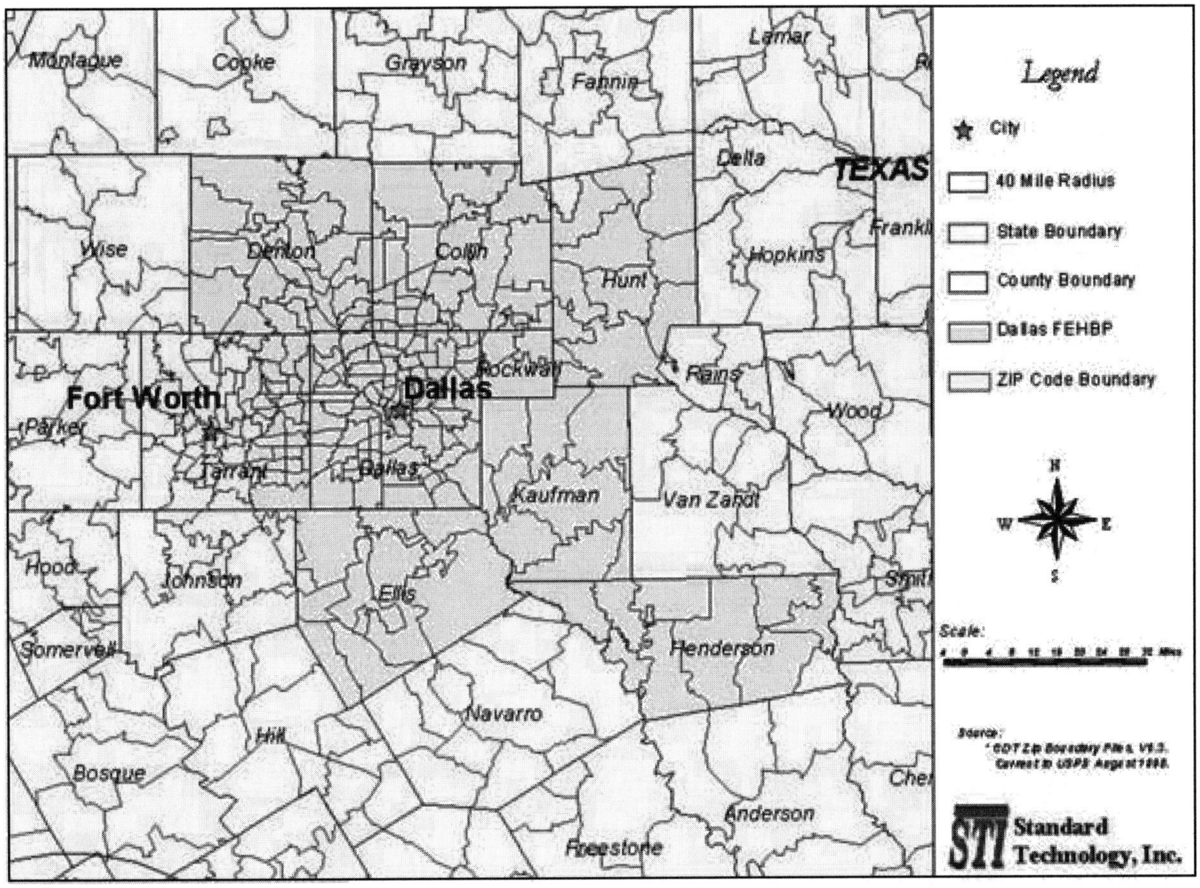

Dallas FEHBP Options

Medical/Surgical Benefits Plans	Type of plan	Service Area	Primary care doctor	Hospital room copay/ insurance	Prescription drugs, generic	Prescription drugs, brand	Monthly: Self only	Monthly: Self & family
			In Network You Pay				Your share of premium	
Aetna U.S. Helathcare	HMO	Dallas/Ft. Worth	$10	0	$5	$10	342.28	684.55
Humana Health Plan of Texas -	HMO	Dalas/Ft. Worth and Austin areas	$10	0	$5	$10	235.12	572.57
NYLCare Health Plan SW	HMO	Dalas/Ft. Worth/East and West Texas	$10	0	$5	$10	176.49	353.00
Pacificare of Texas	HMO	San Antonio/Houston/Glv ston/Dallas/Ft. Worth/Glf Coast	$10	0	$5	$10	256.92	667.95
Texas Health Choice	HMO	Dallas/Ft. Worth	$10	0	$6	$12	278.53	557.05

POS									
APWU Health Plan – Eastern and Central Texas									
Monthly: Self only	Monthly: Self & family	Primary care doctor	Hospital room copay/ insurance	Prescription drugs, generic	Prescription drugs, brand	Primary care doctor office copay	Hospital inpatient R&B charges	Prescription drugs, generic	R/Brand/ Local
Your share of premium		In Network You Pay				Out of Network You Pay			
129.65	278.07	$10	0	20%	20%	30%	30%	40%	40%

FEHBP Quality Ratings

Plan Name	Satisfaction Indicators 1=above average, 2=average, 3=below average							
	Overall plan satisfaction	Getting needed care	Getting care quickly	How well doctors communicate	Courteous and helpful office staff	Customer service	Claims processing	Child survey Overall satisfactoin
Aetna U.S. Helathcare	3	3	3	2	2	3	3	3
Humana Health Plan of Texas -	3	3	2	2	2	3	3	
NYLCare Health Plan SW	3	3	3	3	3	2	2	2
Pacificare of Texas	2	3	2	2	2	2	3	2
Texas Health Choice	2	3	2	3	2	3	2	3
APWU Health Plan	3	3	2	2	3	3	3	3

DALLAS, TX MEDICARE HEALTH PLAN COMPARISONS

	Harris Methodist Health Plan The Senior Health Plan (H4559 - 003)	**NYLCare, an Aetna U.S. Healthcare Company** Medicare 10 (H4507 - 001) Greater Dallas/Ft. Worth	**NYLCare, an Aetna U.S. Healthcare Company** Medicare 5 (H4507 - 002) Gulf Coast Area A	**NYLCare, an Aetna U.S. Healthcare Company** Medicare Premier (H4507 - 003) Greater Dallas/Ft. Worth
Premium (Part B - $45.50/month in 2000)	You pay nothing if you have Medicare Parts A and B.	You pay nothing if you have Medicare Parts A and B.	You pay nothing if you have Medicare Parts A and B.	You pay $27 a month if you have Medicare Parts A and B.
Physician Visits	You pay $7 for each visit with your personal physician.	You pay $10 for each visit with your personal physician.	You pay $5 for each visit with your personal physician.	You pay $5 for each visit with your personal physician.
Inpatient Hospital	You pay nothing for your hospital stay. You are covered for additional days in the hospital. Contact plan for details.	You pay nothing for your hospital stay. You are covered for additional days in the hospital. Contact plan for details.	You pay nothing for your hospital stay. You are covered for additional days in the hospital. Contact plan for details.	You pay nothing for your hospital stay. You are covered for additional days in the hospital. Contact plan for details.
Doctor Choice	You need a referral to see a specialist some of the time. Contact plan for details.	You need a referral to see a specialist some of the time. Contact plan for details.	You need a referral to see a specialist some of the time. Contact plan for details.	You need a referral to see a specialist some of the time. Contact plan for details.

	Harris Methodist Health Plan The Senior Health Plan (H4559 - 003)	**NYLCare, an Aetna U.S. Healthcare Company** Medicare 10 (H4507 - 001) Greater Dallas/Ft. Worth	**NYLCare, an Aetna U.S. Healthcare Company** Medicare 5 (H4507 - 002) Gulf Coast Area A	**NYLCare, an Aetna U.S. Healthcare Company** Medicare Premier (H4507 - 003) Greater Dallas/Ft. Worth
Prescription Drugs	Prescription drugs are covered with limits. You pay $5 per generic prescription. You pay $20 per brand name prescription. You have an unlimited generic drug benefit. Your brand name prescription drugs are covered up to $1,000 per year. You must use plan-approved prescription drugs.	Prescription drugs are covered with limits. You pay $15 per generic prescription. You pay $15 per brand name prescription. Your generic and brand name prescription drugs are covered up to $500 per year. You must use plan-approved prescription drugs. There are other limits on prescription drugs. Contact plan for details.	Prescription drugs are covered with limits. You pay $10 per generic prescription. You pay $20 per brand name prescription. You have an unlimited generic drug benefit. Your brand name prescription drugs are covered up to $1,000 per year. If you do not use plan-approved drugs, your costs may be different. There are other limits on prescription drugs. Contact plan for details.	Prescription drugs are covered with limits. You pay $10 per generic prescription. You pay $20 per brand name prescription. You have an unlimited generic drug benefit. Your brand name prescription drugs are covered up to $1,500 per year. If you do not use plan-approved drugs, your costs may be different. There are other limits on prescription drugs. Contact plan for details.
Physical Exams	You pay $7 for a physical exam. You are covered for 1 physical exam(s) per year.	You pay $10 for a physical exam. You are covered for 1 physical exam(s) per year.	You pay $5 for a physical exam. You are covered for 1 physical exam(s) per year.	You pay $5 for a physical exam. You are covered for 1 physical exam(s) per year.
Vision Services	You have some coverage for glasses, contacts and routine eye exams. Contact plan for details.	You have some coverage for glasses, contacts and routine eye exams. Contact plan for details.	You have some coverage for glasses, contacts and routine eye exams. Contact plan for details.	You have some coverage for glasses, contacts and routine eye exams. Contact plan for details.

	Harris Methodist Health Plan The Senior Health Plan (H4559 - 003)	**NYLCare, an Aetna U.S. Healthcare Company** Medicare 10 (H4507 - 001) Greater Dallas/Ft. Worth	**NYLCare, an Aetna U.S. Healthcare Company** Medicare 5 (H4507 - 002) Gulf Coast Area A	**NYLCare, an Aetna U.S. Healthcare Company** Medicare Premier (H4507 - 003) Greater Dallas/Ft. Worth
Dental	You are covered for some other dental care beyond the basic Medicare benefit. Contact plan for details.	You are covered for some other dental care beyond the basic Medicare benefit. Contact plan for details.	You are covered for some other dental care beyond the basic Medicare benefit. Contact plan for details.	You are covered for some other dental care beyond the basic Medicare benefit. Contact plan for details.

DALLAS, TX MEDICARE HEALTH PLAN COMPARISONS (cont.)

	Pacificare of Texas, Inc. Secure Horizons – Plan Area B – Dallas (H4590-011) Dallas, TX	**Scott and White Health Plan** Scott and White Health Plan (H4564-001) Central Texas	**Scott and White Health Plan** Scott and White Health Plan (H4564-002) Central Texas	**Scott and White Health Plan** Scott and White Health Plan (H4564-003) Central Texas
Premium (Part B - $45.50/month in 2000)	You pay nothing if you have Medicare Parts A and B.	You pay $79 a month if you have Medicare Parts A and B.	You pay $49 a month if you have Medicare Parts A and B.	You pay nothing if you have Medicare Parts A and B.
Physician Visits	You pay $6 for each visit with your personal physician.	You pay nothing to see your personal physician.	You pay nothing to see your personal physician.	You pay $10 for each visit with your personal physician.
Inpatient Hospital	You pay nothing for your hospital stay. You are covered for additional days in the hospital. Contact plan for details.	You pay nothing for your hospital stay. You are covered for additional days in the hospital. Contact plan for details.	You pay nothing for your hospital stay. You are covered for additional days in the hospital. Contact plan for details.	You pay $300 for each admission to a plan hospital.

	Pacificare of Texas, Inc. Secure Horizons – Plan Area B – Dallas (H4590-011) Dallas, TX	**Scott and White Health Plan** Scott and White Health Plan (H4564-001) Central Texas	**Scott and White Health Plan** Scott and White Health Plan (H4564-002) Central Texas	**Scott and White Health Plan** Scott and White Health Plan (H4564-003) Central Texas
Doctor Choice	You need a referral to see a specialist, except for your annual GYN visit.	You need a referral to see a specialist some of the time. Contact plan for details.	You need a referral to see a specialist some of the time. Contact plan for details.	You need a referral to see a specialist some of the time. Contact plan for details.
Prescription Drugs	Prescription drugs are covered with limits. You pay $5 per generic prescription. You pay $25 per brand name prescription. Your generic and brand name prescription drugs are covered up to $1,000 per year. You must use plan-approved prescription drugs. There are other limits on prescription drugs. Contact plan for details.	Prescription drugs are covered with limits. You pay $6 per generic prescription. You pay $15 per brand name prescription. Your prescription drugs are covered up to $600 per year. Contact plan for details on how this limit applies. If you do not use plan-approved drugs, your costs may be different. There is a quarterly limit for prescription drugs. Contact the plan for details.	You pay 100% for most prescription drugs.	You pay 100% for most prescription drugs.
Physical Exams	You pay $6 for a physical exam. You are covered for 1 physical exam(s) per year.	You pay nothing for a physical exam. You are covered an unlimited number of physical exams per year.	You pay nothing for a physical exam. You are covered an unlimited number of physical exams per year.	You pay 100% for routine physical exams.

	Pacificare of Texas, Inc. Secure Horizons – Plan Area B – Dallas (H4590-011) Dallas, TX	**Scott and White Health Plan** Scott and White Health Plan (H4564-001) Central Texas	**Scott and White Health Plan** Scott and White Health Plan (H4564-002) Central Texas	**Scott and White Health Plan** Scott and White Health Plan (H4564-003) Central Texas
Vision Services	You have some coverage for glasses, contacts, and routine eye exams. Contact the plan for details.	You have some coverage for glasses, contacts, and routine eye exams. Contact the plan for details.	You have some coverage for glasses, contacts, and routine eye exams. Contact the plan for details.	Routine eye exams and glasses are not covered. You are covered for diagnostic and therapeutic services for the eye.
Dental	In general, you pay 100% for dental services.	You are covered for 2 preventive dental exam(s) every 1 year(s). You pay nothing per preventive dental exam. You are covered for some other dental care beyond the basic Medicare benefit. Contact plan for details.	In general, you pay 100% for dental services.	In general, you pay 100% for dental services.

DALLAS, TX MEDICARE HEALTH PLAN COMPARISONS (cont.)

	Texas Health Choice Golden Choice (H4578 - 001), Dallas/Ft. Worth	**TRICARE Senior Prime (Military Retirees)** TRICARE Senior Prime (H4586 - 001), Southwest
Premium (Part B - $45.50/month in 2000)	You pay nothing if you have Medicare Parts A and B.	You pay nothing if you have Medicare Parts A and B.
Physician Visits	You pay $5 for each visit with your personal physician.	You pay nothing to see your personal physician.
Inpatient Hospital	You pay nothing for your hospital stay.	You pay nothing for your hospital stay. You are covered for additional days in the hospital. Contact plan for details.
Doctor Choice	You need a referral to see a specialist, except for your annual GYN visit.	You need a referral to see a specialist some of the time. Contact plan for details.
Prescription Drugs	Prescription drugs are covered with limits. You pay $5 per generic prescription. You pay $15 per brand name prescription. You have an unlimited generic drug benefit. Your brand name prescription drugs are covered up to $1,500 per year. If you do not use plan-approved drugs, your costs may be different. There are other limits on prescription drugs. Contact plan for details.	Prescription drugs are covered with limits. You pay nothing per generic prescription. You pay nothing per brand name prescription. You have an unlimited prescription drug benefit. If you do not use plan-approved drugs, your costs may be different.
Physical Exams	You pay $5 for a physical exam. You are covered for 1 physical exam(s) per year.	You pay nothing for a physical exam.
Vision Services	You have some coverage for glasses, contacts and routine eye exams. Contact plan for details.	You have some coverage for routine eye exams. Contact plan for details.
Dental	You are covered for unlimited preventive dental exams per year. You pay $20 per preventive dental exam. You are covered for some other dental care beyond the basic Medicare benefit. Contact plan for details.	In general, you pay 100% for dental services.

DALLAS, TEXAS MEDICARE QUALITY RATINGS

	Satisfaction Indicators			
Plan Name	Overall Rating of Managed Care Plan	Overall Rating of Health Care Patients Received	Doctors Who Communicate Well	Ease of Getting Referrals to a Specialist
Harris Methodist Health Plan	57%	58%	78%	86%
NYLCare, an Aetna U.S. Healthcare Company	53%	51%	71%	81%
NYLCare, an Aetna U.S. Healthcare Company	61%	59%	73%	87%
PacifiCare of Texas, Inc./(Dallas)	51%	56%	73%	80%
Scott and White Health Plan	69%	65%	79%	88%
Texas Health Choice	Data not available	Data not available	Data not available	Data not available
TRICARE Senior Prime (Military Retirees)	Data not available	Data not available	Data not available	Data not available

APPENDIX F

DOVER AIR FORCE BASE, DELAWARE

(includes parts of Delaware and Maryland)

1) **Map of Demonstration Area**
2) **Summary of Local FEHBP Options**
3) **Summary of Medicare+Choice Options**

FEHBP Demonstration: Dover Air Force Base, Delaware

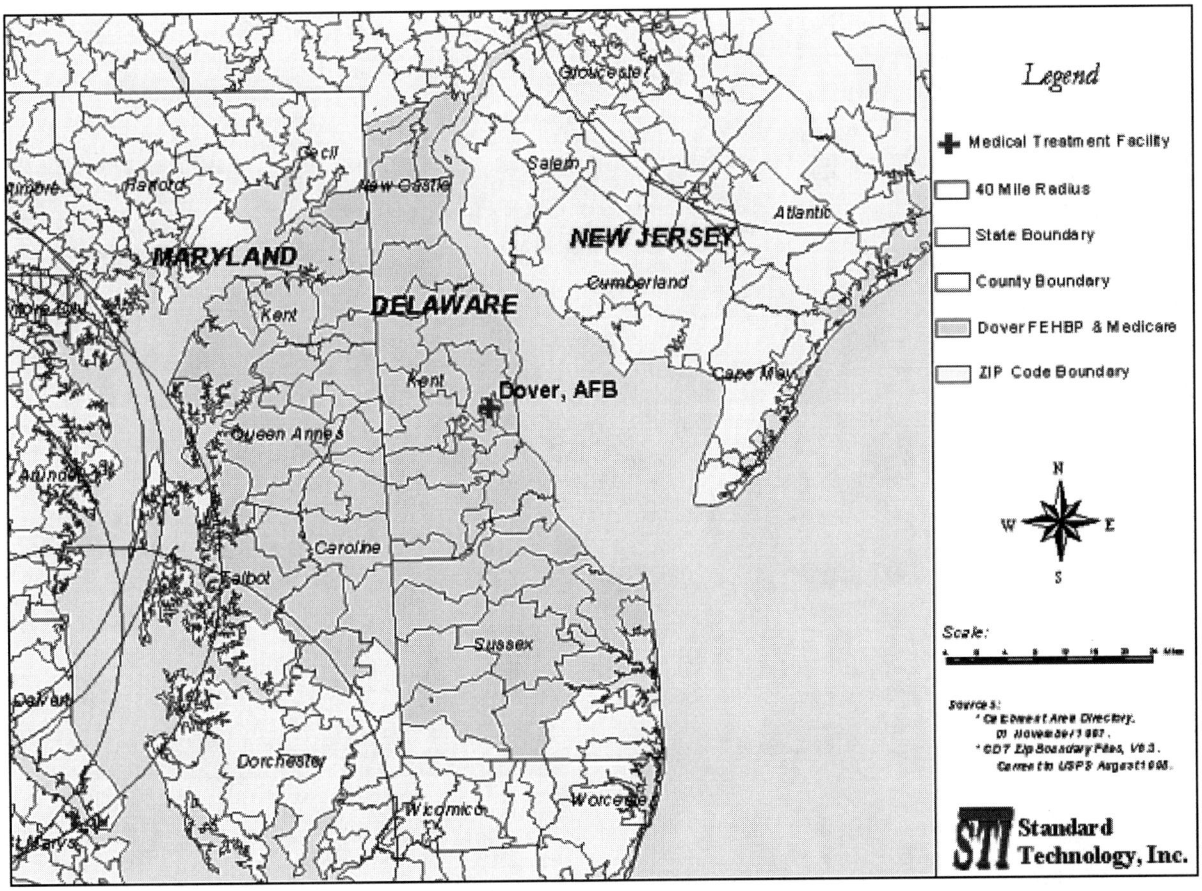

Delaware and Maryland FEHBP Options

Medical/Surgical Benefits Plans	Type of plan	Service Area	Primary care doctor	Hospital room copay/ insurance	Prescription drugs, generic	Prescription drugs, brand	Your share of premium, Monthly: Self only	Your share of premium, Monthly: Self & family
			In Network You Pay					
Aetna U.S. Health Care	HMO	All of Delaware	$10	0	$5	$10	279.87	520.06
MD-IPA	HMO	All of Maryland	$10	0	$5	$10	62.66	116.46
Prudential HelathCare HMO	HMO	Most of Maryland	$10	0	$5	$15	250.92	462.11

			Primary care doctor	Hospital room copay/ insurance	Prescription drugs, generic	Prescription drugs, brand	Primary care doctor office copay	Hospital inpatient R&B charges	Prescription drugs, generic	R/Brand/ Local
			In Network You Pay				Out of Network You Pay			
Free State Health Plan	POS	All of Maryland	$10	0	$10	$20	20%	20%	$10	$20
							Your share of premium, Monthly: Self only		Your share of premium, Monthly: Self & family	
							261.21		482.78	

Delaware and Maryland Quality Ratings

	Satisfaction Indicators 1=above average, 2=average, 3=below average							
Plan Name	Overall plan satisfaction	Getting needed care	Getting care quickly	How well doctors communicate	Courteous and helpful office staff	Customer service	Claims processing	Child survey Overall satisfactoin
Free State Health Plan	2	2	2	1	2	2	2	2
Aetna U.S. Health Care								
Aetna U.S. Healthcare-High	2	2	3	2	3	2	2	1
Aetna U.S. Healthcare- Std	2	2	3	2	3	2	2	1
CapitalCare	2	3	2	2	2	2	1	2
George Washington Univ HP	3	2	3	3	3	3	3	3
MD-IPA	2	2	2	2	2	1	1	2
Prudential HealthCare HMO	3	2	2	2	2	3	3	

DELAWARE MEDICARE HEALTH PLAN COMPARISONS

	Blue Cross Blue Shield of DE, Inc. Medicare Blue (H0803 - 001)	**CIGNA HealthCare of Delaware, Inc.** CIGNA HealthCare for Seniors Premium Plan (H0852 - 001) New Castle County	**Coventry Health Care Of Delaware, Inc.** Advantra (H0802 - 001)	**TRICARE Senior Prime (Military Retirees)** TRICARE Senior Prime (H0853 - 001)	**Freestate Health Plan, Inc.** Medi-CareFirst (H2101 - 002)
Premium (Part B - $45.50/month in 2000)	You pay $60 a month if you have Medicare Parts A and B.	You pay $30 a month if you have Medicare Parts A and B.	You pay $81 a month if you have Medicare Parts A and B.	You pay nothing if you have Medicare Parts A and B.	You pay $50 a month if you have Medicare Parts A and B.
Physician Visits	You pay $5 for each visit with your personal physician.	You pay $10 for each visit with your personal physician.	You pay $10 for each visit with your personal physician.	You pay nothing to see your personal physician.	You pay $5 for each visit with your personal physician.
Inpatient Hospital	You pay nothing for your hospital stay. You are covered for additional days in the hospital. Contact plan for details.	You pay nothing for your hospital stay. You are covered for additional days in the hospital. Contact plan for details.	You pay $100 for each admission to a plan hospital. You are covered for additional days in the hospital. Contact plan for details.	You pay $25 for each admission to a plan hospital. You are covered for additional days in the hospital. Contact plan for details.	You pay nothing for your hospital stay. You are covered for additional days in the hospital. Contact plan for details.
Doctor Choice	You need a referral to see a specialist some of the time. Contact plan for details.	You need a referral to see a specialist some of the time. Contact plan for details.	You need a referral to see a specialist, except for your annual GYN visit.	You need a referral to see a specialist some of the time. Contact plan for details.	You need a referral to see a specialist some of the time. Contact plan for details.

	Blue Cross Blue Shield of DE, Inc. Medicare Blue (H0803 - 001)	**CIGNA HealthCare of Delaware, Inc.** CIGNA HealthCare for Seniors Premium Plan (H0852 - 001) New Castle County	**Coventry Health Care Of Delaware, Inc.** Advantra (H0802 - 001)	**TRICARE Senior Prime (Military Retirees)** TRICARE Senior Prime (H0853 - 001)	**Freestate Health Plan, Inc.** Medi-CareFirst (H2101 - 002)
Prescription Drugs	You pay 100% for most prescription drugs.	Prescription drugs are covered with limits. You pay $7 per generic prescription. You pay $15 per brand name prescription. You have an unlimited generic drug benefit. Your brand name prescription drugs are covered up to $100 per year. You must use plan-approved prescription drugs.	You pay 100% for most prescription drugs.	Prescription drugs are covered with limits. You pay nothing per generic prescription. You pay nothing per brand name prescription. You have an unlimited prescription drug benefit. If you do not use plan-approved drugs, your costs may be different.	Prescription drugs are covered with limits. You pay $15 per generic prescription. You pay $15 per brand name prescription. Your generic and brand name prescription drugs are covered up to $1,000 per year. You must use plan-approved prescription drugs. There are other limits on prescription drugs. Contact plan for details.
Physical Exams	You pay $5 for a physical exam. You are covered for 1 physical exam(s) per year.	You pay $10 for a physical exam. You are covered for 1 physical exam(s) per year.	You pay $10 for a physical exam. You are covered for 1 physical exam(s) per year.	You pay nothing for a physical exam.	You pay $5 for a physical exam. You are covered for an unlimited number of physical exams per year.
Vision Services	You have some coverage for glasses, contacts and routine eye exams. Contact plan for details.	You have some coverage for routine eye exams. Contact plan for details.	Routine eye exams and glasses are not covered. You are covered for diagnostic and therapeutic services for the eye.	You have some coverage for routine eye exams. Contact plan for details.	You have some coverage for glasses, contacts and routine eye exams. Contact plan for details.

	Blue Cross Blue Shield of DE, Inc. Medicare Blue (H0803 - 001)	**CIGNA HealthCare of Delaware, Inc.** CIGNA HealthCare for Seniors Premium Plan (H0852 - 001) New Castle County	**Coventry Health Care Of Delaware, Inc.** Advantra (H0802 - 001)	**TRICARE Senior Prime (Military Retirees)** TRICARE Senior Prime (H0853 - 001)	**Freestate Health Plan, Inc.** Medi-CareFirst (H2101 - 002)
Dental	In general, you pay 100% for dental services.	In general, you pay 100% for dental services.	In general, you pay 100% for dental services.	In general, you pay 100% for dental services.	You are covered for unlimited preventive dental exams per year. You pay $3 per preventive dental exam. You are covered for some other dental care beyond the basic Medicare benefit. Contact plan for details.

MARYLAND MEDICARE HEALTH PLAN COMPARISONS

	Kaiser Fndn Hp of The Mid-Atlantic Sts (H2150 - 999)	**TRICARE Senior Prime (Military Retirees)** TRICARE Senior Prime (H0853 - 001)	**United HealthCare Insurance Company** EverCare (H2155 - 001)
Premium (Part B - $45.50/month in 2000)		You pay nothing if you have Medicare Parts A and B.	You pay nothing if you have Medicare Parts A and B.

	Kaiser Fndn Hp of The Mid-Atlantic Sts (H2150 - 999)	**TRICARE Senior Prime (Military Retirees)** TRICARE Senior Prime (H0853 - 001)	**United HealthCare Insurance Company** EverCare (H2155 - 001)
Physician Visits		You pay nothing to see your personal physician.	You pay nothing to see your personal physician.
Inpatient Hospital		You pay $25 for each admission to a plan hospital. You are covered for additional days in the hospital. Contact plan for details.	You pay nothing for your hospital stay. You are covered for additional days in the hospital. Contact plan for details.
Doctor Choice		You need a referral to see a specialist some of the time. Contact plan for details.	You need a referral to see a specialist some of the time. Contact plan for details.
Prescription Drugs		Prescription drugs are covered with limits. You pay nothing per generic prescription. You pay nothing per brand name prescription. You have an unlimited prescription drug benefit. If you do not use plan-approved drugs, your costs may be different.	You pay 100% for most prescription drugs.
Physical Exams		You pay nothing for a physical exam.	You pay nothing for a physical exam. You are covered for an unlimited number of physical exams per year.
Vision Services		You have some coverage for routine eye exams. Contact plan for details.	Routine eye exams and glasses are not covered. You are covered for diagnostic and therapeutic services for the eye.

	Kaiser Fndn Hp of The Mid-Atlantic Sts (H2150 - 999)	**TRICARE Senior Prime (Military Retirees)** TRICARE Senior Prime (H0853 - 001)	**United HealthCare Insurance Company** EverCare (H2155 - 001)
Dental		In general, you pay 100% for dental services.	In general, you pay 100% for dental services.

DELAWARE MEDICARE QUALITY RATINGS

Plan Name	Satisfaction Indicators			
	Overall Rating of Managed Care Plan	Overall Rating of Health Care Patients Received	Doctors Who Communicate Well	Ease of Getting Referrals to a Specialist
Blue Cross Blue Shield of DE, Inc.	Data not available	Data not available	Data not available	Data not available
CIGNA HealthCare of Delaware, Inc.	Data not available	Data not available	Data not available	Data not available
Coventry Health Care Of Delaware, Inc.	Data not available	Data not available	Data not available	Data not available
TRICARE Senior Prime (Military Retirees)	Data not available	Data not available	Data not available	Data not available

MARYLAND MEDICARE QUALITY RATINGS

Plan Name	Satisfaction Indicators			
	Overall Rating of Managed Care Plan	Overall Rating of Health Care Patients Received	Doctors Who Communicate Well	Ease of Getting Referrals to a Specialist
Kaiser Fndn Hp of The Mid-Atlantic Sts	Data not available	Data not available	Data not available	Data not available
TRICARE Senior Prime (Military Retirees)	Data not available	Data not available	Data not available	Data not available
United HealthCare Insurance Company	Data not available	Data not available	Data not available	Data not available

APPENDIX G

FORT KNOX, KENTUCKY

(includes part of southern Indiana)

1) **Map of Demonstration Area**
2) **Summary of Local FEHBP Options**
3) **Summary of Medicare+Choice Options**

FEHBP Demonstration: Fort Knox, Kentucky

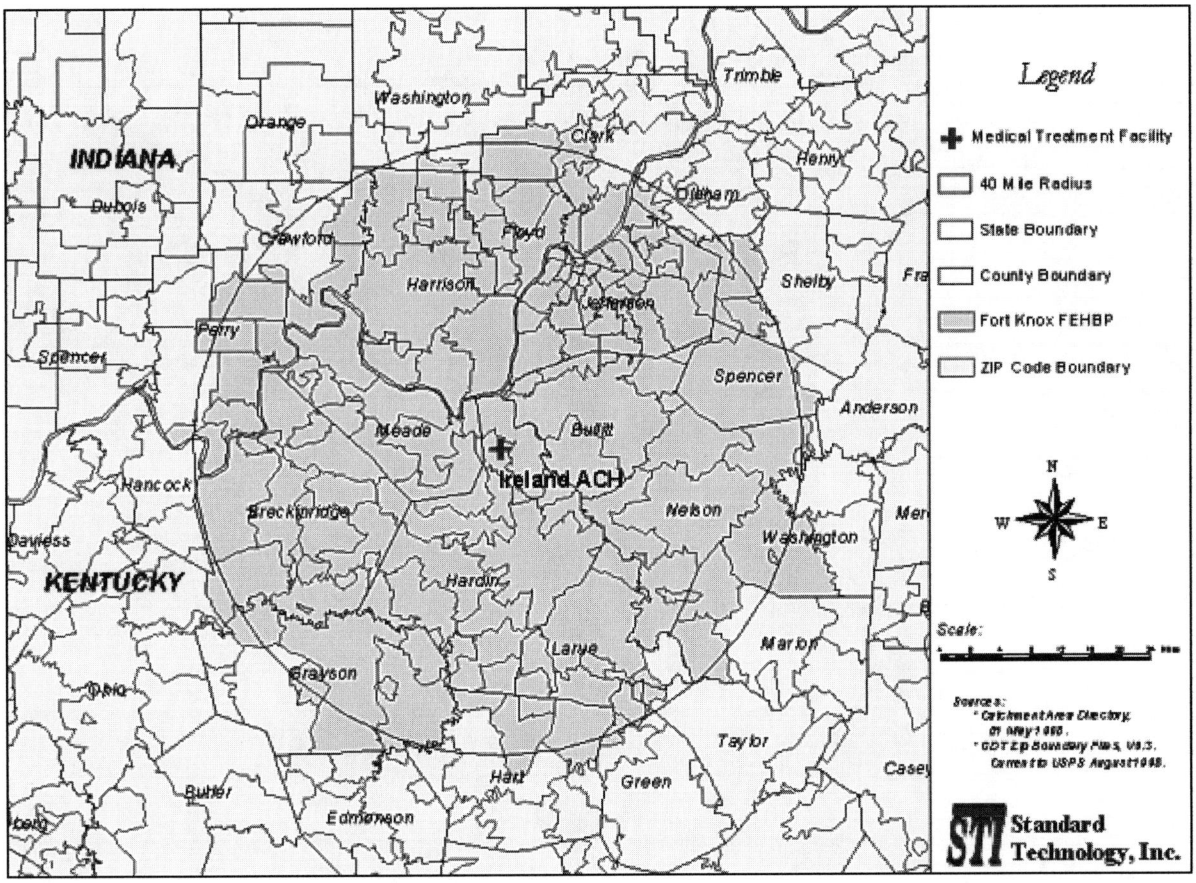

Fort Knox, Kentucky FEHBP Options

Medical/Surgical Benefits Plans	Type of plan	Service Area	Primary care doctor	Hospital room copay/ insurance	Prescription drugs, generic	Prescription drugs, brand	Monthly Self only	Monthly Self & family
			In Network You Pay				Your share of premium	
Aetna U.S. Healthcare	HMO	Lexington/Louisville areas	$10	0	$5	$10	52.69	105.37
Humana Care Plan	HMO	Louisville area	$10	0	$5	$10	80.38	221.54
Humana Health Plan	HMO	Lexington/Louisville	$10	0	$5	$10	80.38	221.54
Aetna U.S. Healthcare	HMO	Southern Indiana	$10	0	$5	$10	52.69	105.37
Humana Care Plan	HMO	Southern Indiana	$10	0	$5	$10	80.38	221.54
Humana Health Plan	HMO	Southern Indiana	$10	0	$5	$10	80.38	221.54
The M*Plan	HMO	Central/Northeast/ Southwest Indiana	$10	0	$5	$10	135.85	262.32

POS											
Bluegrass Family Health Central/Eastern Kentucky											
Biweekly		Monthly		Primary care doctor	Hospital room copay/ insurance	Prescription drugs, generic	Prescription drugs, brand	Primary care doctor office copay	Hospital inpatient R&B charges	Prescription drugs, generic	R/Brand/ Local
Self only	Self & family	Self only	Self & family								
Your share of premium				In Network You Pay				Out of Network You Pay			
28.12	54.52	60.93	118.12	$10	0	$5	$10	30%	0	$5	$10

Fort Knox, Kentucky FEHBP Quality Ratings

Plan Name	Satisfaction Indicators 1=above average, 2=average, 3=below average							
	Overall plan satisfaction	Getting needed care	Getting care quickly	How well doctors communicate	Courteous and helpful office staff	Customer service	Claims processing	Child survey Overall satisfactoin
Advantage Care Inc.	2	2	1	1	1	1	1	2
Aetna U.S. Healthcare	3	3	1	2	2	3	3	2
Humana Care Plan	2	2	1	1	2	3	2	
Humana Care Plan	3	2	3	2	2	3	3	
Humana Health Plan	3	3	2	2	2	3	2	
PacifiCare of Ohio, Inc.	2	2	1	2	1	2	2	2
Prudential HealthCare HMO Midwest	3	2	2	3	2	3	3	
United Health Care of Ohio	2	1	2	2	2	1	2	1
Aetna U.S. Healthcare	3	3	1	2	2	3	3	2
Humana Care Plan	3	2	3	2	2	3	3	
Humana Health Plan	3	3	2	2	2	3	2	
Maxicare Indiana	3	2	2	2	2	3	3	3
The M*Plan	2	2	1	2	2	2	2	2

Fort Knox, Kentucky plans offered in the demonstration site

Company Name	Tel. No.	Plan Benefits									
		A	B	C	D	E	F	G	H	I	J
Anthem Blue Cross/Blue Shield	5024232011	√	√	√					√		
Humana Health Plan Inc.	5025805050	√	√	√			√		√		
Guanrantee Trust Life Insurance Company	8476990600		√	√	√		√				
Mutual of Omaha Insurance Company	4023427600		√	√	√	√	√	√			
Mutual Protective Insurance Company	4023916900	√	√	√	√		√				
Pioneer Life Insurance Company	8159875000		√	√	√		√				
Pyramid Life Insurance Company	9137721110		√	√	√		√	√			
United Healthcare Insurance Company/AARP Health Care Options	2156535007			√							

FORT KNOX, KENTUCKY MEDICARE HEALTH PLAN COMPARISONS

	Anthem Health Plans of Kentucky, Inc. Anthem Senior Advantage-Louisville (H1849 - 002)	**Anthem Health Plans of Kentucky, Inc.** Anthem Senior Advantage-Northern Kentucky (H1849 - 001)	**Humana Health Plan, Inc.** Humana Gold Plus - Louisville Premium (H1890 - 005)	**Humana Health Plan, Inc.** Humana Gold Plus - Louisville Value (H1890 - 003)	**PacifiCare of Ohio, Inc.** Secure Horizons - N. Kentucky (H3658 - 006)
Premium (Part B - $45.50/month in 2000)	You pay $25 a month if you have Medicare Parts A and B.	You pay nothing if you have Medicare Parts A and B.	You pay $111 a month if you have Medicare Parts A and B.	You pay $14 a month if you have Medicare Parts A and B.	You pay $39 a month if you have Medicare Parts A and B.
Physician Visits	You pay $10 for each visit with your personal physician.	You pay $5 for each visit with your personal physician.	You pay $12 for each visit with your personal physician.	You pay $15 for each visit with your personal physician.	You pay $10 for each visit with your personal physician.
Doctor Choice	You need a referral to see a specialist, except for your annual GYN visit.	You need a referral to see a specialist, except for your annual GYN visit.	You need a referral to see a specialist some of the time. Contact plan for details.	You need a referral to see a specialist some of the time. Contact plan for details.	You need a referral to see a specialist some of the time. Contact plan for details.
	Anthem Health Plans of Kentucky, Inc. Anthem Senior Advantage-Louisville (H1849 - 002)	**Anthem Health Plans of Kentucky, Inc.** Anthem Senior Advantage-Northern Kentucky (H1849 - 001)	**Humana Health Plan, Inc.** Humana Gold Plus - Louisville Premium (H1890 - 005)	**Humana Health Plan, Inc.** Humana Gold Plus - Louisville Value (H1890 - 003)	**PacifiCare of Ohio, Inc.** Secure Horizons - N. Kentucky (H3658 - 006)

Prescription Drugs	Prescription drugs are covered with limits. You pay $10 per generic prescription. You pay $25 per brand name prescription. You have an unlimited generic drug benefit. Your brand name prescription drugs are covered up to $600 per year. If you do not use plan-approved drugs, your costs may be different.	Prescription drugs are covered with limits. You pay $10 per generic prescription. You pay $25 per brand name prescription. You have an unlimited generic drug benefit. Your brand name prescription drugs are covered up to $800 per year. If you do not use plan-approved drugs, your costs may be different.	Prescription drugs are covered with limits. You pay $10 per generic prescription. You pay $15 per brand name prescription. Your generic and brand name prescription drugs are covered up to $800 per year. If you do not use plan-approved drugs, your costs may be different. There is a quarterly limit for prescription drugs. Contact plan for details.	You pay 100% for most prescription drugs.	Prescription drugs are covered with limits. You pay $10 per generic prescription. You pay $20 per brand name prescription. You have an unlimited generic drug benefit. Your brand name prescription drugs are covered up to $500 per year. Contact plan for details on how this limit applies. If you do not use plan-approved drugs, your costs may be different. There are other limits on prescription drugs. Contact plan for details.
Vision Services	You have some coverage for routine eye exams. Contact plan for details.	You have some coverage for routine eye exams. Contact plan for details.	Routine eye exams and glasses are not covered. You are covered for diagnostic and therapeutic services for the eye.	Routine eye exams and glasses are not covered. You are covered for diagnostic and therapeutic services for the eye.	You have some coverage for glasses, contacts and routine eye exams. Contact plan for details.
Dental	You are covered for 1 preventive dental exam(s) every 1 year(s). You pay nothing per preventive dental exam.	You are covered for 1 preventive dental exam(s) every 1 year(s). You pay nothing per preventive dental exam.	You are covered for some other dental care beyond the basic Medicare benefit. Contact plan for details.	You are covered for some other dental care beyond the basic Medicare benefit. Contact plan for details.	In general, you pay 100% for dental services.

INDIANA MEDICARE HEALTH PLAN COMPARISONS

	Maxicare Health Plans, Inc. Max65 Plus (H9028 - 004)	**Maxicare Health Plans, Inc.** Max65 Plus (H9028 - 006)	**The MPlan** Senior Smart Choice High Option (H1553 - 002)	**The MPlan** Senior Smart Choice (H1553 - 001)	**Welborn HMO** BASIC PLAN (H1558 - 003)
Premium (Part B - $45.50/month in 2000)	You pay $59 a month if you have Medicare Parts A and B.	You pay $29 a month if you have Medicare Parts A and B.	You pay $52 a month if you have Medicare Parts A and B.	You pay $37 a month if you have Medicare Parts A and B.	You pay $102 a month if you have Medicare Parts A and B.
	Maxicare Health Plans, Inc. Max65 Plus (H9028 - 004)	**Maxicare Health Plans, Inc.** Max65 Plus (H9028 - 006)	**The MPlan** Senior Smart Choice High Option (H1553 - 002)	**The MPlan** Senior Smart Choice (H1553 - 001)	**Welborn HMO** BASIC PLAN (H1558 - 003)
Physician Visits	You pay $10 for each visit with your personal physician.	You pay $10 for each visit with your personal physician.	You pay $8 for each visit with your personal physician.	You pay $8 for each visit with your personal physician.	You pay nothing to see your personal physician.
Inpatient Hospital	You pay $200 for each admission to a plan hospital. You are covered for additional days in the hospital. Contact plan for details.	You pay $200 for each admission to a plan hospital. You are covered for additional days in the hospital. Contact plan for details.	You pay nothing for your hospital stay. You are covered for additional days in the hospital. Contact plan for details.	You pay nothing for your hospital stay.	You pay nothing for your hospital stay. You are covered for additional days in the hospital. Contact plan for details.
Doctor Choice	You need a referral to see a specialist some of the time. Contact plan for details.	You need a referral to see a specialist some of the time. Contact plan for details.	You do not need a referral to see a specialist.	You do not need a referral to see a specialist.	You need a referral to see a specialist, except for your annual GYN visit.

Prescription Drugs	Prescription drugs are covered with limits. You pay $5 per generic prescription. You pay $25 per brand name prescription. Your generic and brand name prescription drugs are covered up to $1,000 per year. You must use plan-approved prescription drugs. There are other limits on prescription drugs. Contact plan for details.	Prescription drugs are covered with limits. You pay $5 per generic prescription. You pay $25 per brand name prescription. Your generic and brand name prescription drugs are covered up to $500 per year. You must use plan-approved prescription drugs. There are other limits on prescription drugs. Contact plan for details.	You pay 100% for most prescription drugs.	You pay 100% for most prescription drugs.	You pay 100% for most prescription drugs.
Physical Exams	You pay $10 for a physical exam. You are covered for 1 physical exam(s) per year.	You pay $10 for a physical exam. You are covered for 1 physical exam(s) per year.	You pay $8 for a physical exam. You are covered for 1 physical exam(s) per year.	You pay $8 for a physical exam. You are covered for 1 physical exam(s) per year.	You pay 100% for routine physical exams.
Vision Services	You have some coverage for glasses, contacts and routine eye exams. Contact plan for details.	Routine eye exams and glasses are not covered. You are covered for diagnostic and therapeutic services for the eye.	You have some coverage for glasses, contacts and routine eye exams. Contact plan for details.	Routine eye exams and glasses are not covered. You are covered for diagnostic and therapeutic services for the eye.	You have some coverage for glasses and contacts. Contact plan for details.
Dental	In general, you pay 100% for dental services.	In general, you pay 100% for dental services.	You are covered for 2 preventive dental exam(s) every 1 year(s). You pay $8 per preventive dental exam. You are covered for some other dental care beyond the basic Medicare benefit. Contact plan for details.	In general, you pay 100% for dental services.	In general, you pay 100% for dental services.

INDIANA MEDICARE HEALTH PLAN COMPARISONS (cont.)

	Welborn HMO Plus Plan (H1558 - 004)
Premium (Part B - $45.50/month in 2000)	You pay $110 a month if you have Medicare Parts A and B.
Physician Visits	You pay nothing to see your personal physician.
Inpatient Hospital	You pay nothing for your hospital stay. You are covered for additional days in the hospital. Contact plan for details.
Doctor Choice	You need a referral to see a specialist, except for your annual GYN visit.
Prescription Drugs	You pay 100% for most prescription drugs.
Physical Exams	You pay nothing for a physical exam. You are covered for an unlimited number of physical exams per year.
Vision Services	You have some coverage for glasses, contacts and routine eye exams. Contact plan for details.
Dental	In general, you pay 100% for dental services.

FORT KNOX, KENTUCKY MEDICARE QUALITY RATINGS

	Satisfaction Indicators			
Plan Name	Overall Rating of Managed Care Plan	Overall Rating of Health Care Patients Received	Doctors Who Communicate Well	Ease of Getting Referrals to a Specialist
Anthem Health Plans of Kentucky, Inc.	Data not available	Data not available	Data not available	Data not available
Humana Health Plan, Inc.	48%	53%	70%	80%
PacifiCare of Ohio, Inc.	48%	60%	75%	89%

APPENDIX H

GREENSBORO/WINSTON-SALEM/HIGH POINT, NORTH CAROLINA

1) **Map of Demonstration Area**
2) **Summary of Local FEHBP Options**
3) **Summary of Medicare+Choice Options**

FEHBP Demonstration: Greensboro/Winston-Salem/High Point, North Carolina

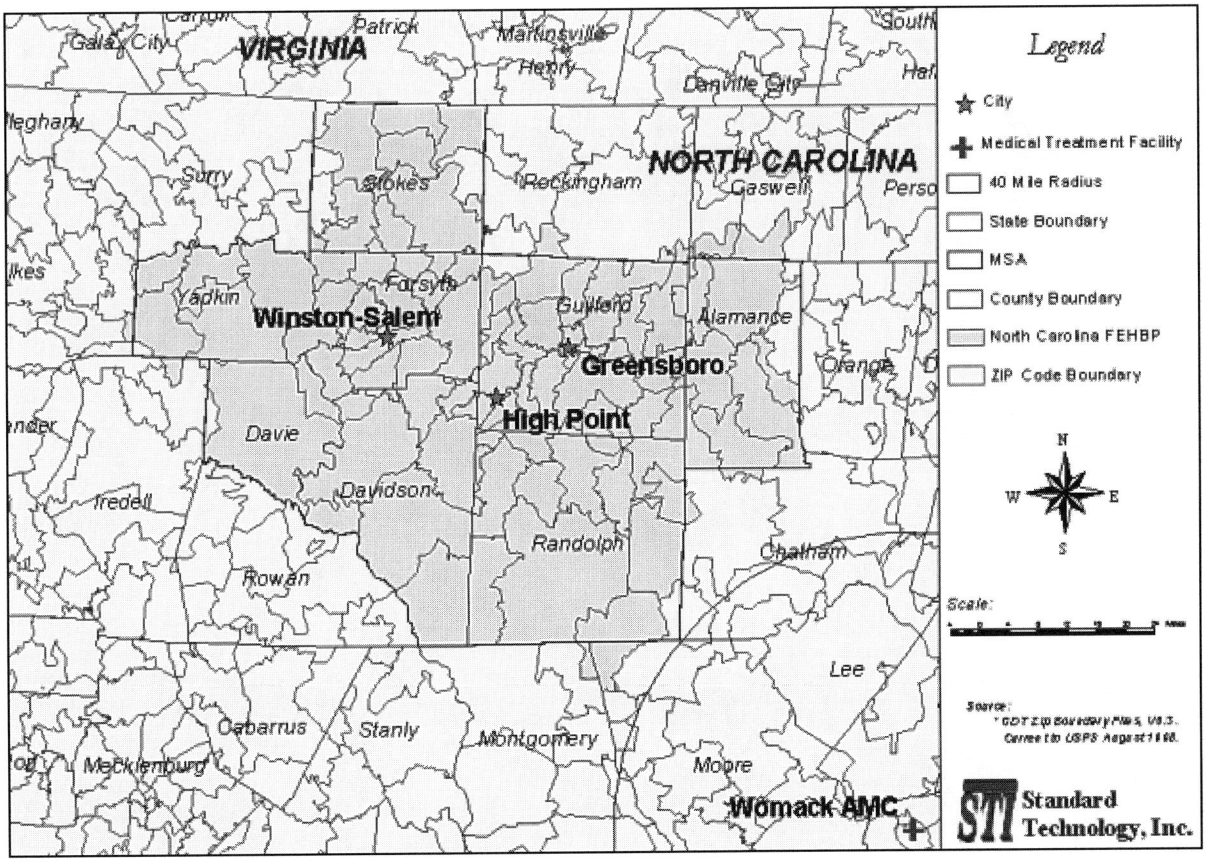

North Carolina FEHBP Plans

Medical/Surgical Benefits Plans	Type of plan	Service Area	Primary care doctor	Hospital room copay/ insurance	Prescription drugs, generic	Prescription drugs, brand	Your share of premium Biweekly Monthly Self only	Self & family
			In Network You Pay					
Partners NHP of NC	HMO	Most of North Carolina	$10	0	$10	$10	54.95	109.88
UHC of North Carolina	HMO	Central/Eastern/Western	$10	0	$10	$15	157.62	359.97

			Primary care doctor	Hospital room copay/ insurance	Prescription drugs, generic	Prescription drugs, brand	Primary care doctor office copay	Hospital inpatient R&B charges	Prescription drugs, generic	R/Brand/ Local
			In Network You Pay				Out of Network You Pay			
QualChoice of North Carolina	POS	Northwestern North Carolina	$10	0	$6	$12	$10	0	$6	$12
							Your share of premium			
							Biweekly		Monthly	
							Self only	Self & family	Self only	Self & family
							24.44	62.02	52.95	134.38

North Carolina FEHBP Quality Ratings

Plan Name	Satisfaction Indicators 1=above average, 2=average, 3=below average							
	Overall plan satisfaction	Getting needed care	Getting care quickly	How well doctors communicate	Courteous and helpful office staff	Customer service	Claims processing	Child survey Overall satisfaction
Aetna U.S. Healthcare	3	3	2	1	1	3	3	3
Doctores Health Plan, Inc	2	2	2	2	2	2	3	2
Generations Family Health Plan	2	2	2	2	2	1	1	
Partners NHP of NC	1	1	1	2	2	1	1	1
Prudential Healthcare HMO	3	3	3	3	3	3	3	3
UHC of North Carolina	1	1	1	2	1	1	1	2

NORTH CAROLINA MEDICARE HEALTH PLAN COMPARISONS

	PARTNERS National Health Plans - NC, Inc. PARTNERS Medicare Choice (H3449 - 004) Winston-Salem	**PARTNERS National Health Plans - NC, Inc.** PARTNERS Medicare Choice (H3449 - 005) Charlotte/Greensboro	**United Healthcare of North Carolina, Inc.** Medicare Complete-- North Carolina (H3456 - 001)
Premium (Part B - $45.50/month in 2000)	You pay $50 a month if you have Medicare Parts A and B.	You pay $50 a month if you have Medicare Parts A and B.	You pay nothing if you have Medicare Parts A and B.
Physician Visits	You pay $15 for each visit with your personal physician.	You pay $15 for each visit with your personal physician.	You pay $20 for each visit with your personal physician.
Inpatient Hospital	You pay nothing for your hospital stay. You are covered for additional days in the hospital. Contact plan for details.	You pay nothing for your hospital stay. You are covered for additional days in the hospital. Contact plan for details.	You pay $250 for each admission to a plan hospital. You are covered for additional days in the hospital. Contact plan for details.
Doctor Choice	You need a referral to see a specialist some of the time. Contact plan for details.	You need a referral to see a specialist some of the time. Contact plan for details.	You need a referral to see a specialist some of the time. Contact plan for details.

	PARTNERS National Health Plans - NC, Inc. PARTNERS Medicare Choice (H3449 - 004) Winston-Salem	**PARTNERS National Health Plans - NC, Inc.** PARTNERS Medicare Choice (H3449 - 005) Charlotte/Greensboro	**United Healthcare of North Carolina, Inc.** Medicare Complete-- North Carolina (H3456 - 001)
Prescription Drugs	Prescription drugs are covered with an additional monthly premium of $25. You pay $10 per generic prescription. You pay $20 per brand name prescription. You have an unlimited generic drug benefit. Your brand name prescription drugs are covered up to $400 per year. If you do not use plan-approved drugs, your costs may be different. There is a quarterly and other limits for prescription drugs. Contact plan for details.	You pay 100% for most prescription drugs.	You pay 100% for most prescription drugs.
Physical Exams	You pay $15 for a physical exam. You are covered for 1 physical exam(s) per year.	You pay $15 for a physical exam. You are covered for 1 physical exam(s) per year.	You pay $20 for a physical exam. You are covered for 1 physical exam(s) per year.
Vision Services	You have some coverage for glasses and routine eye exams. Contact plan for details.	You have some coverage for glasses and routine eye exams. Contact plan for details.	You have some coverage for routine eye exams. Contact plan for details.
Dental	In general, you pay 100% for dental services.	In general, you pay 100% for dental services.	In general, you pay 100% for dental services.

NORTH CAROLINA MEDICARE QUALITY RATINGS

	Satisfaction Indicators			
Plan Name	Overall Rating of Managed Care Plan	Overall Rating of Health Care Patients Received	Doctors Who Communicate Well	Ease of Getting Referrals to a Specialist
PARTNERS National Health Plans	59%	64%	78%	90%
QualChoice of North Carolina, Inc.	66%	58%	73%	87%
United Healthcare of North Carolina, Inc.	Data not available	Data not available	Data not available	Data not available

APPENDIX I

HUMBOLDT COUNTY, CALIFORNIA

1) **Map of Demonstration Area**
2) **Summary of Local FEHBP Options**
3) **Summary of Medicare+Choice Options**

FEHBP Demonstration: Humboldt County, California

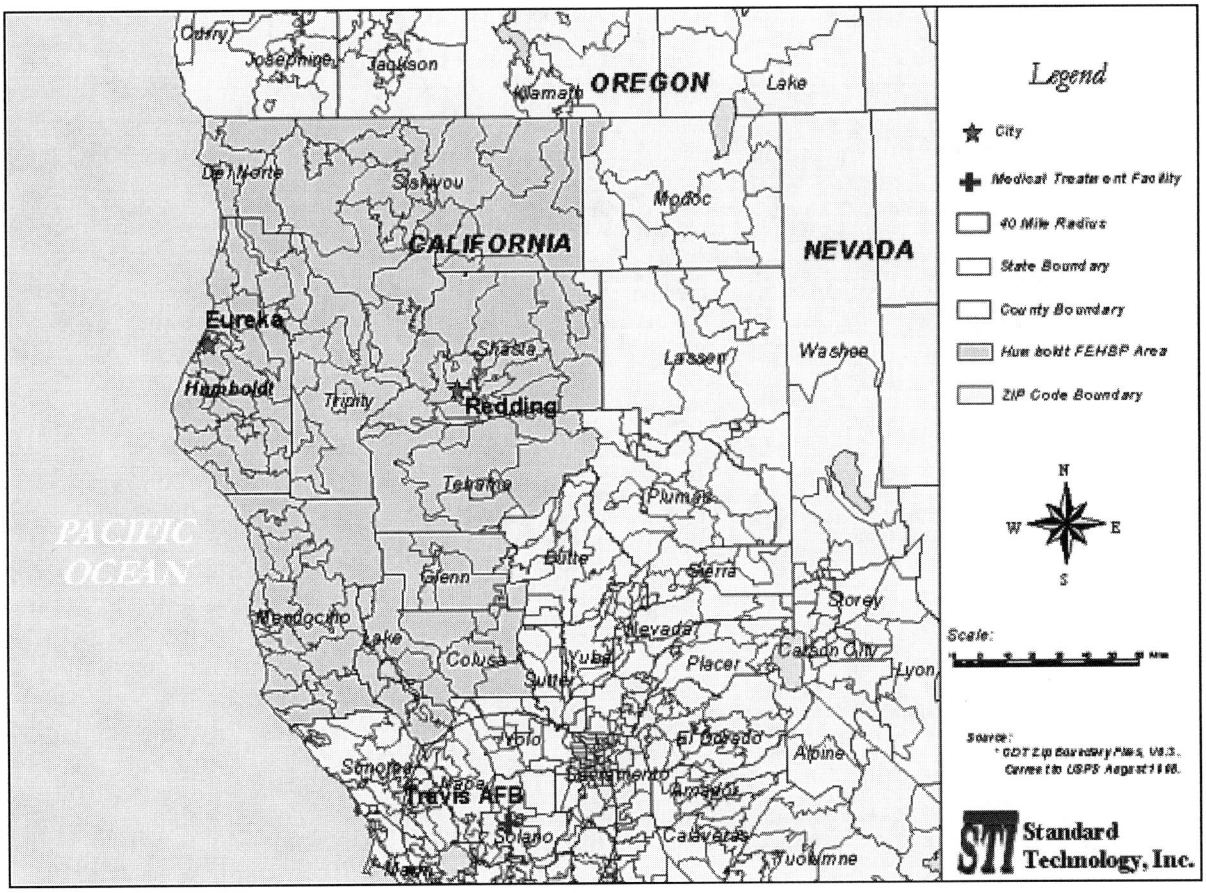

Humboldt County, California FEHBP Options

Medical/Surgical Benefits Plans	Type of plan	Service Area	Primary care doctor	Hospital room copay/ insurance	Prescription drugs, generic	Prescription drugs, brand	Biweekly Self only	Biweekly Self & family	Monthly Self only	Monthly Self & family
			In Network You Pay				Your share of premium			
Aetna U.S. Healthcare	HMO	Northern California	$10	0	$5	$10	33.92	76.51	73.49	165.77
Blue Shield of CA Access+HMO	HMO	Most of California	$10	0	$6	$6	20.49	50.83	44.39	110.14
CaliforniaCare	HMO	Most of California	$10	0	$5	$10	22.57	57.59	48.90	124.77
CIGNA HealthCare of California	HMO	Northern/Southern California	$10	0	$5	$10	22.60	49.73	48.97	107.75
Health Net	HMO	Most of California	$10	0	$5	$10	20.42	48.35	44.25	104.75
Kaiser Permanente	HMO	Northern California	$10	0	$5	$5	21.67	51.72	46.95	112.07
National HMO Health Plan	HMO	Northern/Central/ Southern California	$10	0	$5	$10	15.50	40.88	33.59	88.57
PacifiCare of California	HMO	Most of California	$10	0	$5	$10	19.46	48.30	42.16	104.65
Western Health Advantage	HMO	Northern California	$10	0	$5	$10	19.57	46.96	42.40	101.76

Humboldt County, CA FEHBP Quality Ratings

Plan Name	Satisfaction Indicators 1=above average, 2=average, 3=below average							
	Overall plan satisfaction	Getting needed care	Getting care quickly	How well doctors communicate	Courteous and helpful office staff	Customer service	Claims processing	Child survey Overall satisfactoin
Aetna U.S. Healthcare	3	3	3	3	3	3	3	2
Blue Shield of CA Access+HMO	3	3	3	3	3	2	3	3
CaliforniaCare	3	3	3	3	3	2	1	2
CIGNA HealthCare of California	3	3	3	3	3	3	3	2
Health Net	2	3	2	3	3	2	2	2
Kaiser Permanente	2	2	2	3	2	2	2	2
National HMO Health Plan								
PacifiCare of California	2	3	3	3	3	2	2	2
Western Health Advantage								

Medigap

Company Name	Tel. No.	Plan Benefits									
		A	B	C	D	E	F	G	H	I	J
AARP Prudential Insurance	800-523-5800	✓	✓	✓	✓	✓	✓	✓	✓	✓	✓
Academy Life Insurance	800-345-6352	✓	✓	✓	✓	✓	✓	✓	✓	✓	✓
AID Association for Lutherans	800-225-5225	✓		✓	✓		✓		✓	✓	
American Life & Health Insurance	800-338-7634	✓			✓				✓		
Bankers Like and Casualty	714-898-2796	✓	✓	✓	✓	✓	✓	✓			
Blue Cross of California	800-333-3883	✓		✓			✓				✓
Blue Shield of California	800-431-2809	✓			✓		✓		✓	✓	
Calfarm Life Insurance	800-444-7140	✓		✓			✓				✓
Celtic Life Insurance	800-766-2525	✓	✓	✓			✓			✓	
Central States Health & Life	800-541-2363	✓	✓	✓			✓				
Combined Insurance Co. of America	800-544-5531	✓		✓			✓				
G.E. Life & Annuity Assurance Co.	800-253-0856	✓		✓	✓		✓				✓
Harvest Life Insurance	800-253-0856	✓		✓	✓		✓				
Medico Life Insurance	800-228-6080	✓		✓			✓	✓			
Mennonite Mutual Aid Association	800-348-7468	✓				✓	✓			✓	
Mutual of Omaha	310-208-5554	✓	✓	✓	✓		✓				
Mutual Protective Insurance	800-228-6080	✓		✓			✓	✓			✓
Pioneer Life Insurance	800-759-7007	✓	✓	✓	✓	✓	✓	✓		✓	
Standard Life and Accident	800-537-8102	✓	✓	✓			✓				
Union Fidelity Life	800-523-5758	✓	✓			✓					
Union Labor Life Insurance	800-368-5724	✓		✓							
United American Insurance	800-825-6767	✓	✓	✓	✓		✓	✓			
USAA Life Insurance	800-531-8000	✓			✓		✓	✓			

HUMBOLDT COUNTY, CALIFORNIA MEDICARE HEALTH PLAN COMPARISONS

	Aetna U.S. Healthcare Medicare 10 (H0547 - 001)	**Aetna U.S. Healthcare** Medicare 5 (H0547 - 002)	**Aetna U.S. Healthcare** Premier (H0547 - 003)	**Aetna U.S. Healthcare** Medicare 10 (H0547 - 004)	**Aetna U.S. Healthcare** Medicare 5 (H0547 - 005)
Premium (Part B - $45.50/month in 2000)	You pay $10 a month if you have Medicare Parts A and B.	You pay $35 a month if you have Medicare Parts A and B.	You pay $65 a month if you have Medicare Parts A and B.	You pay $20 a month if you have Medicare Parts A and B.	You pay $50 a month if you have Medicare Parts A and B.
Physician Visits	You pay $10 for each visit with your personal physician.	You pay $5 for each visit with your personal physician.	You pay $5 for each visit with your personal physician.	You pay $10 for each visit with your personal physician.	You pay $5 for each visit with your personal physician.
Inpatient Hospital	You pay nothing for your hospital stay. You are covered for additional days in the hospital. Contact plan for details.	You pay nothing for your hospital stay. You are covered for additional days in the hospital. Contact plan for details.	You pay nothing for your hospital stay. You are covered for additional days in the hospital. Contact plan for details.	You pay nothing for your hospital stay. You are covered for additional days in the hospital. Contact plan for details.	You pay nothing for your hospital stay. You are covered for additional days in the hospital. Contact plan for details.
Doctor Choice	You need a referral to see a specialist some of the time. Contact plan for details.	You need a referral to see a specialist some of the time. Contact plan for details.	You need a referral to see a specialist some of the time. Contact plan for details.	You need a referral to see a specialist some of the time. Contact plan for details.	You need a referral to see a specialist some of the time. Contact plan for details.

	Aetna U.S. Healthcare Medicare 10 (H0547 - 001)	**Aetna U.S. Healthcare** Medicare 5 (H0547 - 002)	**Aetna U.S. Healthcare** Premier (H0547 - 003)	**Aetna U.S. Healthcare** Medicare 10 (H0547 - 004)	**Aetna U.S. Healthcare** Medicare 5 (H0547 - 005)
Prescription Drugs	Prescription drugs are covered with limits. You pay $10 per generic prescription. You pay $20 per brand name prescription. Your generic and brand name prescription drugs are covered up to $500 per year. If you do not use plan-approved drugs, your costs may be different. There are other limits on prescription drugs. Contact plan for details.	Prescription drugs are covered with limits. You pay $10 per generic prescription. You pay $20 per brand name prescription. You have an unlimited generic drug benefit. Your brand name prescription drugs are covered up to $1,000 per year. If you do not use plan-approved drugs, your costs may be different. There are other limits on prescription drugs. Contact plan for details.	Prescription drugs are covered with limits. You pay $5 per generic prescription. You pay $15 per brand name prescription. You have an unlimited generic drug benefit. Your brand name prescription drugs are covered up to $1,000 per year. If you do not use plan-approved drugs, your costs may be different. There are other limits on prescription drugs. Contact plan for details.	Prescription drugs are covered with limits. You pay $10 per generic prescription. You pay $20 per brand name prescription. Your generic and brand name prescription drugs are covered up to $500 per year. If you do not use plan-approved drugs, your costs may be different. There are other limits on prescription drugs. Contact plan for details.	Prescription drugs are covered with limits. You pay $10 per generic prescription. You pay $20 per brand name prescription. You have an unlimited generic drug benefit. Your brand name prescription drugs are covered up to $1,000 per year. If you do not use plan-approved drugs, your costs may be different. There are other limits on prescription drugs. Contact plan for details.
Physical Exams	You pay $10 for a physical exam. You are covered for 1 physical exam(s) per year.	You pay $5 for a physical exam. You are covered for 1 physical exam(s) per year.	You pay $5 for a physical exam. You are covered for 1 physical exam(s) per year.	You pay $10 for a physical exam. You are covered for 1 physical exam(s) per year.	You pay $5 for a physical exam. You are covered for 1 physical exam(s) per year.

	Aetna U.S. Healthcare Medicare 10 (H0547 - 001)	**Aetna U.S. Healthcare** Medicare 5 (H0547 - 002)	**Aetna U.S. Healthcare** Premier (H0547 - 003)	**Aetna U.S. Healthcare** Medicare 10 (H0547 - 004)	**Aetna U.S. Healthcare** Medicare 5 (H0547 - 005)
Vision Services	You have some coverage for glasses, contacts and routine eye exams. Contact plan for details.	You have some coverage for glasses, contacts and routine eye exams. Contact plan for details.	You have some coverage for glasses, contacts and routine eye exams. Contact plan for details.	You have some coverage for glasses, contacts and routine eye exams. Contact plan for details.	You have some coverage for glasses, contacts and routine eye exams. Contact plan for details.
Dental	You are covered for some other dental care beyond the basic Medicare benefit. Contact plan for details.	You are covered for some other dental care beyond the basic Medicare benefit. Contact plan for details.	You are covered for 2 preventive dental exam(s) every 1 year(s). You pay $5 per preventive dental exam. You are covered for some other dental care beyond the basic Medicare benefit. Contact plan for details.	You are covered for some other dental care beyond the basic Medicare benefit. Contact plan for details.	You are covered for some other dental care beyond the basic Medicare benefit. Contact plan for details.

HUMBOLDT COUNTY, CALIFORNIA MEDICARE HEALTH PLAN COMPARISONS (cont.)

	Aetna U.S. Healthcare Premier (H0547 - 006)	**Aetna U.S. Healthcare** Medicare 10 (H0547 - 007)	**Aetna U.S. Healthcare** Medicare 5 (H0547 - 008)	**Aetna U.S. Healthcare** Premier (H0547 - 009)	**Kaiser Permanente Health Plan, Inc.** Kaiser Permanente Senior Advantage (H0583 - 001)
Premium (Part B - $45.50/month in 2000)	You pay $80 a month if you have Medicare Parts A and B.	You pay $40 a month if you have Medicare Parts A and B.	You pay $70 a month if you have Medicare Parts A and B.	You pay $100 a month if you have Medicare Parts A and B.	You pay nothing if you have Medicare Parts A and B.
Physician Visits	You pay $5 for each visit with your personal physician.	You pay $10 for each visit with your personal physician.	You pay $5 for each visit with your personal physician.	You pay $5 for each visit with your personal physician.	You pay $10 for each visit with your personal physician.
Inpatient Hospital	You pay nothing for your hospital stay. You are covered for additional days in the hospital. Contact plan for details.	You pay nothing for your hospital stay. You are covered for additional days in the hospital. Contact plan for details.	You pay nothing for your hospital stay. You are covered for additional days in the hospital. Contact plan for details.	You pay nothing for your hospital stay. You are covered for additional days in the hospital. Contact plan for details.	You pay nothing for your hospital stay. You are covered for additional days in the hospital. Contact plan for details.
Doctor Choice	You need a referral to see a specialist some of the time. Contact plan for details.	You need a referral to see a specialist some of the time. Contact plan for details.	You need a referral to see a specialist some of the time. Contact plan for details.	You need a referral to see a specialist some of the time. Contact plan for details.	You need a referral to see a specialist some of the time. Contact plan for details.

	Aetna U.S. Healthcare Premier (H0547 - 006)	**Aetna U.S. Healthcare** Medicare 10 (H0547 - 007)	**Aetna U.S. Healthcare** Medicare 5 (H0547 - 008)	**Aetna U.S. Healthcare** Premier (H0547 - 009)	**Kaiser Permanente Health Plan, Inc.** Kaiser Permanente Senior Advantage (H0583 - 001)
Prescription Drugs	Prescription drugs are covered with limits. You pay $5 per generic prescription. You pay $15 per brand name prescription. You have an unlimited generic drug benefit. Your brand name prescription drugs are covered up to $1,000 per year. If you do not use plan-approved drugs, your costs may be different. There are other limits on prescription drugs. Contact plan for details.	Prescription drugs are covered with limits. You pay $10 per generic prescription. You pay $20 per brand name prescription. Your generic and brand name prescription drugs are covered up to $500 per year. If you do not use plan-approved drugs, your costs may be different. There are other limits on prescription drugs. Contact plan for details.	Prescription drugs are covered with limits. You pay $10 per generic prescription. You pay $20 per brand name prescription. You have an unlimited generic drug benefit. Your brand name prescription drugs are covered up to $1,000 per year. If you do not use plan-approved drugs, your costs may be different. There are other limits on prescription drugs. Contact plan for details.	Prescription drugs are covered with limits. You pay $5 per generic prescription. You pay $15 per brand name prescription. You have an unlimited generic drug benefit. Your brand name prescription drugs are covered up to $1,000 per year. If you do not use plan-approved drugs, your costs may be different. There are other limits on prescription drugs. Contact plan for details.	Prescription drugs are covered with limits. You pay $10 per generic prescription. You pay $10 per brand name prescription. Your generic and brand name prescription drugs are covered up to $1,600 per year. You must use plan-approved prescription drugs.
Physical Exams	You pay $5 for a physical exam. You are covered for 1 physical exam(s) per year.	You pay $10 for a physical exam. You are covered for 1 physical exam(s) per year.	You pay $5 for a physical exam. You are covered for 1 physical exam(s) per year.	You pay $5 for a physical exam. You are covered for 1 physical exam(s) per year.	You pay $10 for a physical exam. You are covered for an unlimited number of physical exams per year.

	Aetna U.S. Healthcare Premier (H0547 - 006)	**Aetna U.S. Healthcare** Medicare 10 (H0547 - 007)	**Aetna U.S. Healthcare** Medicare 5 (H0547 - 008)	**Aetna U.S. Healthcare** Premier (H0547 - 009)	**Kaiser Permanente Health Plan, Inc.** Kaiser Permanente Senior Advantage (H0583 - 001)
Vision Services	You have some coverage for glasses, contacts and routine eye exams. Contact plan for details.	You have some coverage for glasses, contacts and routine eye exams. Contact plan for details.	You have some coverage for glasses, contacts and routine eye exams. Contact plan for details.	You have some coverage for glasses, contacts and routine eye exams. Contact plan for details.	You have some coverage for glasses, contacts and routine eye exams. Contact plan for details.
Dental	You are covered for 2 preventive dental exam(s) every 1 year(s). You pay $5 per preventive dental exam. You are covered for some other dental care beyond the basic Medicare benefit. Contact plan for details.	You are covered for some other dental care beyond the basic Medicare benefit. Contact plan for details.	You are covered for some other dental care beyond the basic Medicare benefit. Contact plan for details.	You are covered for 2 preventive dental exam(s) every 1 year(s). You pay $5 per preventive dental exam. You are covered for some other dental care beyond the basic Medicare benefit. Contact plan for details.	In general, you pay 100% for dental services.

HUMBOLDT COUNTY, CALIFORNIA MEDICARE QUALITY RATINGS

	Satisfaction Indicators			
Plan Name	Overall Rating of Managed Care Plan	Overall Rating of Health Care Patients Received	Doctors Who Communicate Well	Ease of Getting Referrals to a Specialist
Aetna U.S. Healthcare	40%	50%	70%	79%
Kaiser Permanente Health Plan, Inc./(Sacramento)	45%	41%	67%	75%

APPENDIX J

NAVAL HOSPITAL, CAMP PENDLETON, CALIFORNIA

1) **Map of Demonstration Area**
2) **Summary of Local FEHBP Options**
3) **Summary of Medicare+Choice Options**

FEHBP Demonstration: Naval Hospital, Camp Pendleton, California

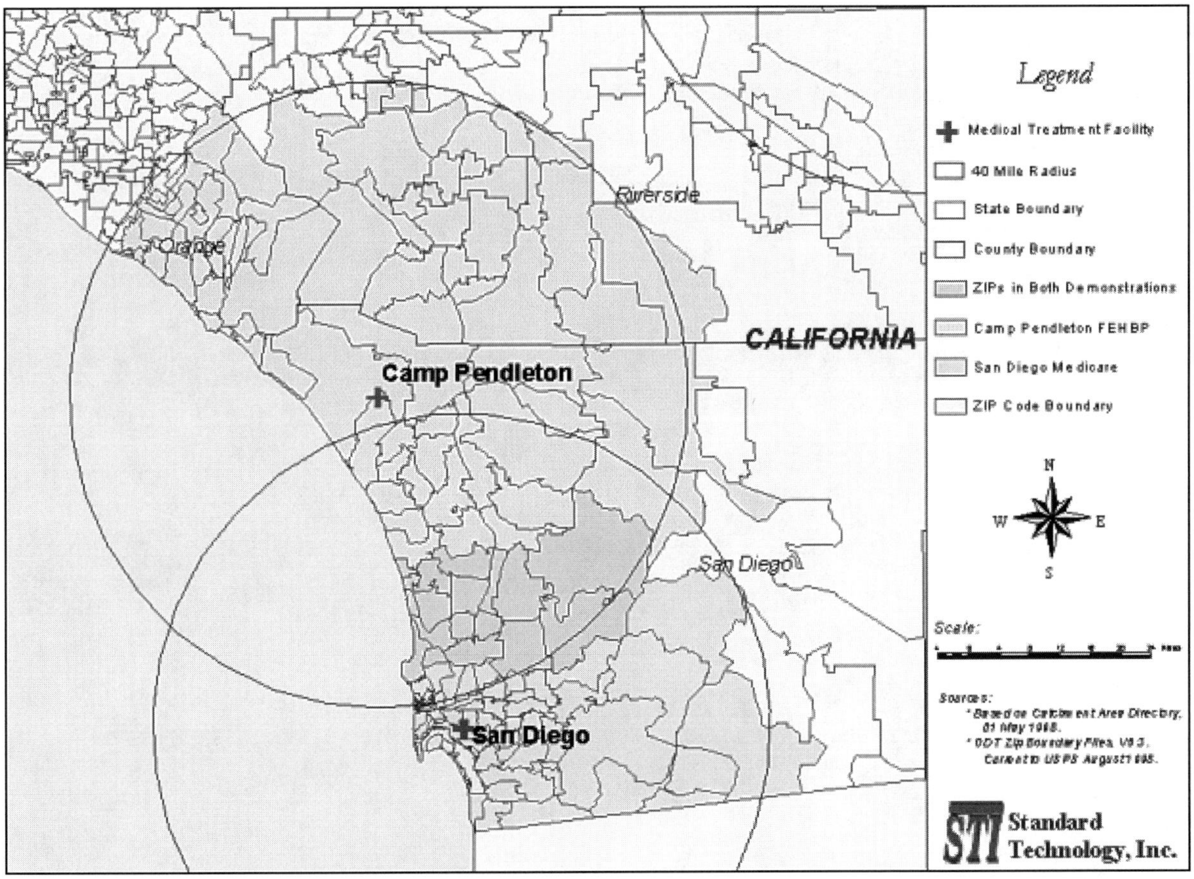

Naval Hospital, Camp Pendleton - California FEHBP Plans

Medical/Surgical Benefits Plans	Type of plan	Service Area	Primary care doctor	Hospital room copay/ insurance	Prescription drugs, generic	Prescription drugs, brand	Biweekly Self only	Biweekly Self & family	Monthly Self only	Monthly Self & family
			In Network You Pay				Your share of premium			
Aetna U.S. Healthcare	HMO	Southern California	$10	0	$5	$10	20.19	47.15	43.75	102.16
Blue Shield of CA Access+HMO	HMO	Most of California	$10	0	$6	$6	20.49	50.83	44.39	110.14
CaliforniaCare	HMO	Most of California	$10	0	$5	$10	22.57	57.59	48.90	124.77
CIGNA HealthCare of California	HMO	Northern/Southern California	$10	0	$5	$10	22.60	49.73	48.97	107.75
Health Net	HMO	Most of California	$10	0	$5	$10	20.42	48.35	44.25	104.75
Kaiser Permanente	HMO	Southern California	$10	0	$5	$5	23.27	53.79	50.43	116.55
Maxicare Southern California	HMO	Southern California	$10	0	$5	$10	18.42	46.81	39.92	101.42
National HMO Health Plan	HMO	Northern/Central/ Southern California	$10	0	$5	$10	15.50	40.88	33.59	88.57
PacifiCare of California	HMO	Most of California	$10	0	$5	$10	19.46	48.30	42.16	104.65
United Health Plan	HMO	LA/Orange/San Bernardino Counties	$10	0	$5	$5	16.95	36.12	36.72	78.25
Universal Care	HMO	Southern California	$10	0	$5	$5	18.19	43.66	39.42	94.61

Naval Hospital, Camp Pendleton - California FEHBP Quality Ratings

Plan Name	Satisfaction Indicators 1=above average, 2=average, 3=below average							
	Overall plan satisfaction	Getting needed care	Getting care quickly	How well doctors communicate	Courteous and helpful office staff	Customer service	Claims processing	Child survey Overall satisfactoin
Aetna U.S. Healthcare	3	3	3	3	3	2	2	2
Blue Shield of CA Access+HMO	3	3	3	3	3	2	3	3
CaliforniaCare	3	3	3	3	3	2	1	2
CIGNA HealthCare of California	3	3	3	3	3	3	3	2
Health Net	2	3	2	3	3	2	2	2
Kaiser Permanente	1	1	3	3	2	2	2	1
Maxicare Southern California	3	3	3	3	3	2	2	2
National HMO Health Plan								
PacifiCare of California	2	3	3	3	3	2	2	2
United Health Plan								
Universal Care								

SOUTHERN CALIFORNIA MEDICARE HEALTH PLAN COMPARISONS

	Aetna U.S. Healthcare Medicare 10 (H0523 - 004) San Diego	**Aetna U.S. Healthcare** Medicare 5 (H0523 - 005) San Diego	**Aetna U.S. Healthcare** Premier (H0523 - 006) San Diego	**Blue Cross of California** Senior Secure (H0564 - 003) Santa Barbara	**Blue Shield of California, Inc.** Blue Shield 65 Plus (H0504 - 007) San Diego
Premium (Part B - $45.50/month in 2000)	You pay nothing if you have Medicare Parts A and B.	You pay $25 a month if you have Medicare Parts A and B.	You pay $60 a month if you have Medicare Parts A and B.	You pay $20 a month if you have Medicare Parts A and B.	You pay nothing if you have Medicare Parts A and B.
Physician Visits	You pay $10 for each visit with your personal physician.	You pay $5 for each visit with your personal physician.	You pay $5 for each visit with your personal physician.	You pay $5 for each visit with your personal physician.	You pay nothing to see your personal physician.
Inpatient Hospital	You pay nothing for your hospital stay. You are covered for additional days in the hospital. Contact plan for details.	You pay nothing for your hospital stay. You are covered for additional days in the hospital. Contact plan for details.	You pay nothing for your hospital stay. You are covered for additional days in the hospital. Contact plan for details.	You pay nothing for your hospital stay. You are covered for additional days in the hospital. Contact plan for details.	You pay nothing for your hospital stay. You are covered for additional days in the hospital. Contact plan for details.
Doctor Choice	You need a referral to see a specialist some of the time. Contact plan for details.	You need a referral to see a specialist some of the time. Contact plan for details.	You need a referral to see a specialist some of the time. Contact plan for details.	You need a referral to see a specialist some of the time. Contact plan for details.	You need a referral to see a specialist, except for your annual GYN visit.

	Aetna U.S. Healthcare Medicare 10 (H0523 - 004) San Diego	**Aetna U.S. Healthcare** Medicare 5 (H0523 - 005) San Diego	**Aetna U.S. Healthcare** Premier (H0523 - 006) San Diego	**Blue Cross of California** Senior Secure (H0564 - 003) Santa Barbara	**Blue Shield of California, Inc.** Blue Shield 65 Plus (H0504 - 007) San Diego
Prescription Drugs	Prescription drugs are covered with limits. You pay $10 per generic prescription. You pay $20 per brand name prescription. Your generic and brand name prescription drugs are covered up to $500 per year. If you do not use plan-approved drugs, your costs may be different. There are other limits on prescription drugs. Contact plan for details.	Prescription drugs are covered with limits. You pay $10 per generic prescription. You pay $20 per brand name prescription. You have an unlimited generic drug benefit. Your brand name prescription drugs are covered up to $2,000 per year. If you do not use plan-approved drugs, your costs may be different. There are other limits on prescription drugs. Contact plan for details.	Prescription drugs are covered with limits. You pay $5 per generic prescription. You pay $10 per brand name prescription. You have an unlimited generic drug benefit. Your brand name prescription drugs are covered up to $2,000 per year. If you do not use plan-approved drugs, your costs may be different. There are other limits on prescription drugs. Contact plan for details.	Prescription drugs are covered with limits. You pay $7 per generic prescription. You pay $25 per brand name prescription. You have an unlimited generic drug benefit. Your brand name prescription drugs are covered up to $500 per year. If you do not use plan-approved drugs, your costs may be different. There are other limits on prescription drugs. Contact plan for details.	Prescription drugs are covered with limits. You pay $5 per generic prescription. You pay $15 per brand name prescription. You have an unlimited prescription drug benefit. You must use plan-approved prescription drugs. There are other limits on prescription drugs. Contact plan for details.
Physical Exams	You pay $10 for a physical exam. You are covered for 1 physical exam(s) per year.	You pay $5 for a physical exam. You are covered for 1 physical exam(s) per year.	You pay $5 for a physical exam. You are covered for 1 physical exam(s) per year.	You pay $5 for a physical exam. You are covered for an unlimited number of physical exams per year.	You pay nothing for a physical exam. You are covered for 1 physical exam(s) per year.
Vision Services	You have some coverage for glasses, contacts and routine eye exams. Contact plan for details.	You have some coverage for glasses, contacts and routine eye exams. Contact plan for details.	You have some coverage for glasses, contacts and routine eye exams. Contact plan for details.	You have some coverage for glasses, contacts and routine eye exams. Contact plan for details.	You have some coverage for glasses and routine eye exams. Contact plan for details.

	Aetna U.S. Healthcare Medicare 10 (H0523 - 004) San Diego	**Aetna U.S. Healthcare** Medicare 5 (H0523 - 005) San Diego	**Aetna U.S. Healthcare** Premier (H0523 - 006) San Diego	**Blue Cross of California** Senior Secure (H0564 - 003) Santa Barbara	**Blue Shield of California, Inc.** Blue Shield 65 Plus (H0504 - 007) San Diego
Dental	You are covered for some other dental care beyond the basic Medicare benefit. Contact plan for details.	You are covered for some other dental care beyond the basic Medicare benefit. Contact plan for details.	You are covered for 2 preventive dental exam(s) every 1 year(s). You pay $5 per preventive dental exam. You are covered for some other dental care beyond the basic Medicare benefit. Contact plan for details.	You are covered for 1 preventive dental exam(s) every 1 year(s). You pay $30 per preventive dental exam. You are covered for some other dental care beyond the basic Medicare benefit. Contact plan for details.	You are covered for 2 preventive dental exam(s) every 1 year(s). You pay $5 per preventive dental exam. You are covered for some other dental care beyond the basic Medicare benefit. Contact plan for details.

SOUTHERN CALIFORNIA MEDICARE HEALTH PLAN COMPARISONS (cont.)

	Blue Shield of California, Inc. Blue Shield 65 Plus (H0504 - 006) San Bernadino	**CIGNA HealthCare of California, Inc.** CIGNA HealthCare for Seniors $0 Individual (H0581 - 001)Riverside	**Health Net** Health Net Seniority Plus (H0562 - 002) Riverside, San Bernadino. San Diego	**Health Net** Health Net Seniority Plus (H0562 - 012) Santa Barbara	**Health Net** Health Net Seniority Plus (H0562 - 017) San Diego
Premium (Part B - $45.50/month in 2000)	You pay nothing if you have Medicare Parts A and B.	You pay nothing if you have Medicare Parts A and B.	You pay nothing if you have Medicare Parts A and B.	You pay $30 a month if you have Medicare Parts A and B.	You pay $75 a month if you have Medicare Parts A and B.
Physician Visits	You pay nothing to see your personal physician.	You pay nothing to see your personal physician.	You pay $5 for each visit with your personal physician.	You pay $10 for each visit with your personal physician.	You pay $15 for each visit with your personal physician.

	Blue Shield of California, Inc. Blue Shield 65 Plus (H0504 - 006) San Bernadino	**CIGNA HealthCare of California, Inc.** CIGNA HealthCare for Seniors $0 Individual (H0581 - 001)Riverside	**Health Net** Health Net Seniority Plus (H0562 - 002) Riverside, San Bernadino. San Diego	**Health Net** Health Net Seniority Plus (H0562 - 012) Santa Barbara	**Health Net** Health Net Seniority Plus (H0562 - 017) San Diego
Doctor Choice	You need a referral to see a specialist, except for your annual GYN visit.	You need a referral to see a specialist some of the time. Contact plan for details.	You need a referral to see a specialist some of the time. Contact plan for details.	You need a referral to see a specialist some of the time. Contact plan for details.	You need a referral to see a specialist some of the time. Contact plan for details.
Prescription Drugs	Prescription drugs are covered with limits. You pay $5 per generic prescription. You pay $15 per brand name prescription. You have an unlimited prescription drug benefit. You must use plan-approved prescription drugs. There are other limits on prescription drugs. Contact plan for details.	Prescription drugs are covered with limits. You pay $7 per generic prescription. You pay 50% per brand name prescription. You have an unlimited generic drug benefit. Your brand name prescription drugs are covered up to $1,000 per year. If you do not use plan-approved drugs, your costs may be different.	Prescription drugs are covered with limits. You pay $5 per generic prescription. You pay $20 per brand name prescription. Your prescription drugs are covered up to $2,000 per year. Contact plan for details on how this limit applies. You must use plan-approved prescription drugs.	Prescription drugs are covered with limits. You pay $6 per generic prescription. You pay $25 per brand name prescription. Your prescription drugs are covered up to $1,000 per year. Contact plan for details on how this limit applies. You must use plan-approved prescription drugs.	Prescription drugs are covered with limits. You pay $6 per generic prescription. You pay 100% per brand name prescription. You have an unlimited prescription drug benefit. You must use plan-approved prescription drugs.
Physical Exams	You pay nothing for a physical exam. You are covered for 1 physical exam(s) per year.	You pay nothing for a physical exam. You are covered for 1 physical exam(s) per year.	You pay $5 for a physical exam. You are covered for 1 physical exam(s) per year.	You pay $10 for a physical exam. You are covered for 1 physical exam(s) per year.	You pay $15 for a physical exam. You are covered for 1 physical exam(s) per year.

	Blue Shield of California, Inc. Blue Shield 65 Plus (H0504 - 006) San Bernadino	**CIGNA HealthCare of California, Inc.** CIGNA HealthCare for Seniors $0 Individual (H0581 - 001)Riverside	**Health Net** Health Net Seniority Plus (H0562 - 002) Riverside, San Bernadino. San Diego	**Health Net** Health Net Seniority Plus (H0562 - 012) Santa Barbara	**Health Net** Health Net Seniority Plus (H0562 - 017) San Diego
Dental	You are covered for 2 preventive dental exam(s) every 1 year(s). You pay $5 per preventive dental exam. You are covered for some other dental care beyond the basic Medicare benefit. Contact plan for details.	You are covered for 2 preventive dental exam(s) every 1 year(s). You pay $5 per preventive dental exam. You are covered for some other dental care beyond the basic Medicare benefit. Contact plan for details.	You are covered for 1 preventive dental exam(s) every 1 year(s). You pay nothing per preventive dental exam. You are covered for some other dental care beyond the basic Medicare benefit. Contact plan for details.	In general, you pay 100% for dental services.	In general, you pay 100% for dental services.

	Kaiser Permanente Health Plan, Inc. Kaiser Permanente Senior Advantage (H0524 - 001) Southern CA	**PacifiCare of California, Inc.** Secure Horizons-Santa Barbara-Standard Pla (H0559 - 002)	**PacifiCare of California, Inc.** Secure Horizons - Orange County Standard (H0543 - 004)	**PacifiCare of California, Inc.** Secure Horizons - Orange County Basic (H0543 - 026)	**PacifiCare of California, Inc.** Secure Horizons-San Luis Obispo-Standard (H0559 - 005)
Premium (Part B - $45.50/month in 2000)	You pay nothing if you have Medicare Parts A and B.	You pay $50 a month if you have Medicare Parts A and B.	You pay nothing if you have Medicare Parts A and B.	You pay nothing if you have Medicare Parts A and B.	You pay $55 a month if you have Medicare Parts A and B.

	Kaiser Permanente Health Plan, Inc. Kaiser Permanente Senior Advantage (H0524 - 001) Southern CA	**PacifiCare of California, Inc.** Secure Horizons-Santa Barbara-Standard Pla (H0559 - 002)	**PacifiCare of California, Inc.** Secure Horizons - Orange County Standard (H0543 - 004)	**PacifiCare of California, Inc.** Secure Horizons - Orange County Basic (H0543 - 026)	**PacifiCare of California, Inc.** Secure Horizons-San Luis Obispo-Standard (H0559 - 005)
Inpatient Hospital	You pay nothing for your hospital stay. You are covered for additional days in the hospital. Contact plan for details.	You pay nothing for your hospital stay. You are covered for additional days in the hospital. Contact plan for details.	You pay nothing for your hospital stay. You are covered for additional days in the hospital. Contact plan for details.	You pay nothing for your hospital stay. You are covered for additional days in the hospital. Contact plan for details.	You pay nothing for your hospital stay. You are covered for additional days in the hospital. Contact plan for details.
Doctor Choice	You need a referral to see a specialist some of the time. Contact plan for details.	You need a referral to see a specialist some of the time. Contact plan for details.	You need a referral to see a specialist some of the time. Contact plan for details.	You need a referral to see a specialist some of the time. Contact plan for details.	You need a referral to see a specialist some of the time. Contact plan for details.
Prescription Drugs	Prescription drugs are covered with limits. You pay $10 per generic prescription. You pay $10 per brand name prescription. You have an unlimited prescription drug benefit. You must use plan-approved prescription drugs.	Prescription drugs are covered with limits. You pay $7 per generic prescription. You pay $25 per brand name prescription. You have an unlimited generic drug benefit. Your brand name prescription drugs are covered up to $1,500 per year. If you do not use plan-approved drugs, your costs may be different. There are other limits on prescription drugs. Contact plan for details.	Prescription drugs are covered with limits. You pay $7 per generic prescription. You pay $15 per brand name prescription. You have an unlimited generic drug benefit. Your brand name prescription drugs are covered up to $2,000 per year. If you do not use plan-approved drugs, your costs may be different. There are other limits on prescription drugs. Contact plan for details.	Prescription drugs are covered with limits. You pay $7 per generic prescription. You pay $15 per brand name prescription. You have an unlimited generic drug benefit. Your brand name prescription drugs are covered up to $2,000 per year. If you do not use plan-approved drugs, your costs may be different. There are other limits on prescription drugs. Contact plan for details.	Prescription drugs are covered with limits. You pay $7 per generic prescription. You pay $25 per brand name prescription. You have an unlimited generic drug benefit. Your brand name prescription drugs are covered up to $1,500 per year. If you do not use plan-approved drugs, your costs may be different. There are other limits on prescription drugs. Contact plan for details.

	Kaiser Permanente Health Plan, Inc. Kaiser Permanente Senior Advantage (H0524 - 001) Southern CA	**PacifiCare of California, Inc.** Secure Horizons-Santa Barbara-Standard Pla (H0559 - 002)	**PacifiCare of California, Inc.** Secure Horizons - Orange County Standard (H0543 - 004)	**PacifiCare of California, Inc.** Secure Horizons - Orange County Basic (H0543 - 026)	**PacifiCare of California, Inc.** Secure Horizons-San Luis Obispo-Standard (H0559 - 005)
Vision Services	You have some coverage for glasses, contacts and routine eye exams. Contact plan for details.	You have some coverage for glasses, contacts and routine eye exams. Contact plan for details.	You have some coverage for glasses, contacts and routine eye exams. Contact plan for details.	You have some coverage for glasses, contacts and routine eye exams. Contact plan for details.	You have some coverage for glasses, contacts and routine eye exams. Contact plan for details.
Dental	In general, you pay 100% for dental services.	In general, you pay 100% for dental services.	You are covered for 4 preventive dental exam(s) every 1 year(s). You pay $5 per preventive dental exam. You are covered for some other dental care beyond the basic Medicare benefit. Contact plan for details.	In general, you pay 100% for dental services.	In general, you pay 100% for dental services.

SOUTHERN CALIFORNIA MEDICARE HEALTH PLAN COMPARISONS (cont.)

	PacifiCare of California, Inc. Secure Horizons - San Bernardino Basic (H0543 - 028)	**PacifiCare of California, Inc.** Secure Horizons - San Bernardino Standard (H0543 - 010)	**PacifiCare of California, Inc.** Secure Horizons - San Diego Basic (H0543 - 029)	**PacifiCare of California, Inc.** Secure Horizons - San Diego Standard (H0543 - 013)	**SCAN(tm) Health Plan** Medicare + Choice Benefit Plan (H9104 - 006) Southern CA
Premium (Part B - $45.50/month in 2000)	You pay nothing if you have Medicare Parts A and B.	You pay nothing if you have Medicare Parts A and B.	You pay $15 a month if you have Medicare Parts A and B.	You pay $15 a month if you have Medicare Parts A and B.	You pay nothing if you have Medicare Parts A and B.
Physician Visits	You pay $10 for each visit with your personal physician.	You pay $10 for each visit with your personal physician.	You pay $5 for each visit with your personal physician.	You pay $5 for each visit with your personal physician.	You pay nothing to see your personal physician.
Inpatient Hospital	You pay nothing for your hospital stay. You are covered for additional days in the hospital. Contact plan for details.	You pay nothing for your hospital stay. You are covered for additional days in the hospital. Contact plan for details.	You pay nothing for your hospital stay. You are covered for additional days in the hospital. Contact plan for details.	You pay nothing for your hospital stay. You are covered for additional days in the hospital. Contact plan for details.	You pay nothing for your hospital stay. You are covered for additional days in the hospital. Contact plan for details.
Doctor Choice	You need a referral to see a specialist some of the time. Contact plan for details.	You need a referral to see a specialist some of the time. Contact plan for details.	You need a referral to see a specialist some of the time. Contact plan for details.	You need a referral to see a specialist some of the time. Contact plan for details.	You need a referral to see a specialist, except for your annual GYN visit.

	PacifiCare of California, Inc. Secure Horizons - San Bernardino Basic (H0543 - 028)	**PacifiCare of California, Inc.** Secure Horizons - San Bernardino Standard (H0543 - 010)	**PacifiCare of California, Inc.** Secure Horizons - San Diego Basic (H0543 - 029)	**PacifiCare of California, Inc.** Secure Horizons - San Diego Standard (H0543 - 013)	**SCAN(tm) Health Plan** Medicare + Choice Benefit Plan (H9104 - 006) Southern CA
Physical Exams	You pay $10 for a physical exam. You are covered for 1 physical exam(s) per year.	You pay $10 for a physical exam. You are covered for 1 physical exam(s) per year.	You pay $5 for a physical exam. You are covered for 1 physical exam(s) per year.	You pay $5 for a physical exam. You are covered for 1 physical exam(s) per year.	You pay nothing for a physical exam. You are covered for an unlimited number of physical exams per year.
Vision Services	You have some coverage for glasses, contacts and routine eye exams. Contact plan for details.	You have some coverage for glasses, contacts and routine eye exams. Contact plan for details.	You have some coverage for glasses, contacts and routine eye exams. Contact plan for details.	You have some coverage for glasses, contacts and routine eye exams. Contact plan for details.	You have some coverage for glasses, contacts and routine eye exams. Contact plan for details.
Dental	In general, you pay 100% for dental services.	You are covered for 4 preventive dental exam(s) every 1 year(s). You pay $5 per preventive dental exam. You are covered for some other dental care beyond the basic Medicare benefit. Contact plan for details.	In general, you pay 100% for dental services.	You are covered for 4 preventive dental exam(s) every 1 year(s). You pay $5 per preventive dental exam. You are covered for some other dental care beyond the basic Medicare benefit. Contact plan for details.	You are covered for 2 preventive dental exam(s) every 1 year(s). You pay $8 per preventive dental exam. You are covered for some other dental care beyond the basic Medicare benefit. Contact plan for details.

SOUTHERN CALIFORNIA MEDICARE HEALTH PLAN COMPARISONS (cont.)

	TRICARE Senior Prime (Military Retirees) TRICARE Senior Prime (H0533 - 002) Southern CA	**UHP Healthcare** UHP Healthcare for Seniors (H9016 - 002) Southern CA
Premium (Part B - $45.50/month in 2000)	You pay nothing if you have Medicare Parts A and B.	You pay nothing if you have Medicare Parts A and B.
Physician Visits	You pay nothing to see your personal physician.	You pay nothing to see your personal physician.
Inpatient Hospital	You pay nothing for your hospital stay. You are covered for additional days in the hospital. Contact plan for details.	You pay nothing for your hospital stay. You are covered for additional days in the hospital. Contact plan for details.
Doctor Choice	You need a referral to see a specialist some of the time. Contact plan for details.	You need a referral to see a specialist, except for your annual GYN visit.
Prescription Drugs	Prescription drugs are covered with limits. You pay nothing per generic prescription. You pay nothing per brand name prescription. You have an unlimited prescription drug benefit. If you do not use plan-approved drugs, your costs may be different.	Prescription drugs are covered with limits. You pay nothing per generic prescription. You pay $5 per brand name prescription. Your generic and brand name prescription drugs are covered up to $3,600 per year. You must use plan-approved prescription drugs. There is a monthly limit for prescription drugs. Contact plan for details.
Physical Exams	You pay nothing for a physical exam.	You pay nothing for a physical exam.
Vision Services	You have some coverage for routine eye exams. Contact plan for details.	You have some coverage for glasses and routine eye exams. Contact plan for details.
Dental	In general, you pay 100% for dental services.	You are covered for some other dental care beyond the basic Medicare benefit. Contact plan for details.

NAVAL HOSPITAL, CAMP PENDLETON, CALIFORNIA MEDICARE QUALITY RATINGS

	Satisfaction Indicators			
Plan Name	Overall Rating of Managed Care Plan	Overall Rating of Health Care Patients Received	Doctors Who Communicate Well	Ease of Getting Referrals to a Specialist
Aetna U.S. Healthcare	45%	48%	62%	78%
Blue Cross of California	40%	38%	64%	69%
CIGNA HealthCare of California, Inc.	34%	39%	63%	78%
Health Net/(San Diego)	36%	39%	66%	78%
Kaiser Foundation Hp, Inc.	Data not available	Data not available	Data not available	Data not available
PacifiCare of California, Inc./(San Diego)	49%	50%	72%	78%
PacifiCare of California, Inc./(Santa Barbara)	49%	46%	68%	76%
SCAN(tm) Health Plan	44%	37%	61%	70%
TRICARE Senior Prime (Military Retirees)	Data not available	Data not available	Data not available	Data not available
UHP Healthcare	43%	40%	64%	69%

APPENDIX K

NEW ORLEANS, LOUISIANA

1) Map of Demonstration Area
2) Summary of Local FEHBP Options
3) Summary of Medicare+Choice Options

FEHBP Demonstration: New Orleans, Louisiana

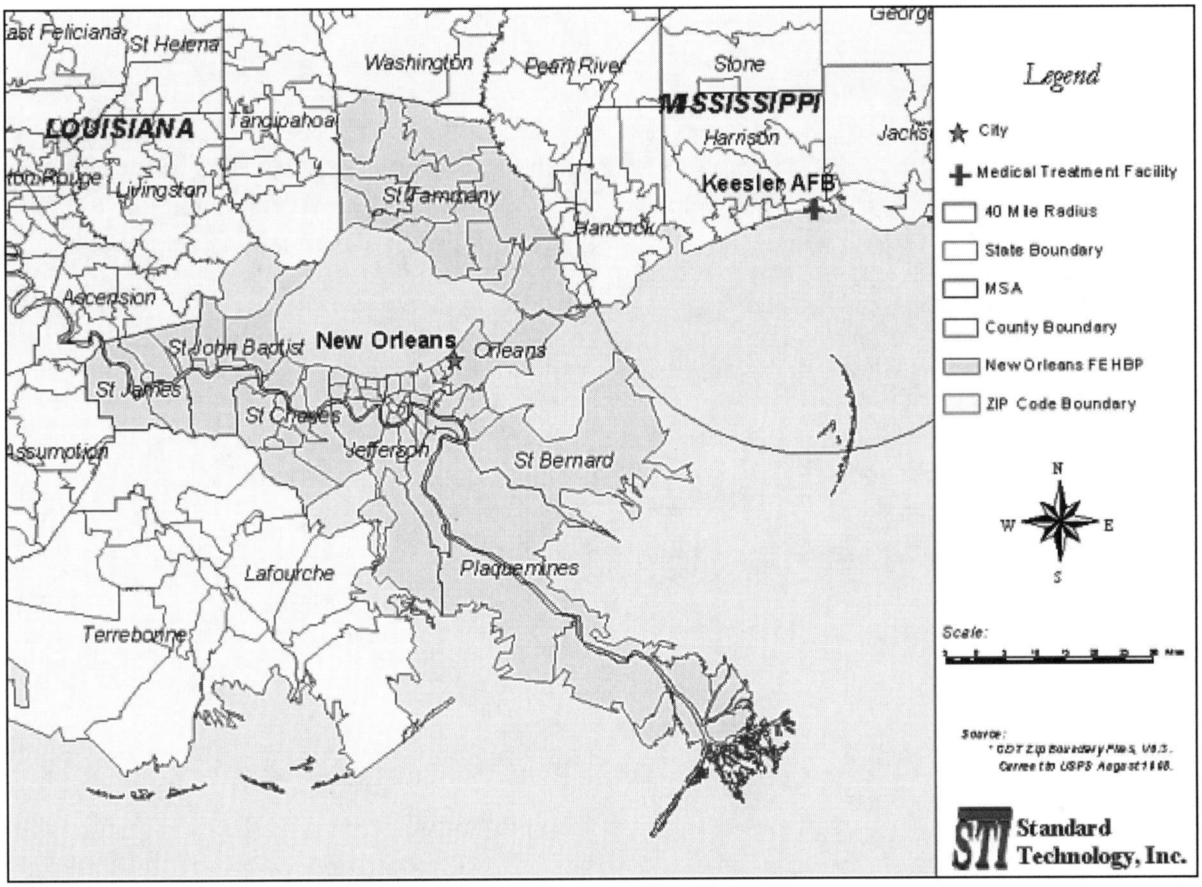

New Orleans, LA FEHBP Options

Medical/Surgical Benefits Plans	Type of plan	Service Area	Primary care doctor (In Network You Pay)	Hospital room copay/ insurance (In Network You Pay)	Prescription drugs, generic (In Network You Pay)	Prescription drugs, brand (In Network You Pay)	Monthly premium Self only	Monthly premium Self & family
Aetna U.S. Healthcare	HMO	New Orleans Area	$10	0	$5	$10	53.39	106.78

POS										
Blue Cross and Blue Shield STD New Orleans area										
Monthly premium Self only	Monthly premium Self & family	Primary care doctor (In Network You Pay)	Hospital room copay/ insurance (In Network You Pay)	Prescription drugs, generic (In Network You Pay)	Prescription drugs, brand (In Network You Pay)	Primary care doctor office copay (Out of Network You Pay)	Hospital inpatient R&B charges (Out of Network You Pay)	Prescription drugs, generic (Out of Network You Pay)	R/Brand/ Local (Out of Network You Pay)	
65.09	144.69	$10	0	$5	$15	25%	30%	45%	45%	
Maxicare Louisiana Baton Rouge/New Orleans area										
Monthly premium Self only	Monthly premium Self & family	Primary care doctor (In Network You Pay)	Hospital room copay/ insurance (In Network You Pay)	Prescription drugs, generic (In Network You Pay)	Prescription drugs, brand (In Network You Pay)	Primary care doctor office copay (Out of Network You Pay)	Hospital inpatient R&B charges (Out of Network You Pay)	Prescription drugs, generic (Out of Network You Pay)	R/Brand/ Local (Out of Network You Pay)	
49.18	102.89	$10	0	$7	$12	20%	20%	N/A	N/A	

New Orleans, LA FEHBP Quality Ratings

	Satisfaction Indicators 1=above average, 2=average, 3=below average							
Plan Name	Overall plan satisfaction	Getting needed care	Getting care quickly	How well doctors communicate	Courteous and helpful office staff	Customer service	Claims processing	Child survey Overall satisfactoin
Blue Cross and Blue Shield STD	2	1	1	2	2	2	3	2
Maxicare Louisiana	2	2	3	2	3	2	3	2

LOUISIANA MEDICARE HEALTH PLAN COMPARISON NOT AVAILABLE AT THIS TIME.

NEW ORLEANS, LOUISIANA MEDICARE QUALITY RATINGS

	Satisfaction Indicators			
Plan Name	Overall Rating of Managed Care Plan	Overall Rating of Health Care Patients Received	Doctors Who Communicate Well	Ease of Getting Referrals to a Specialist
Aetna U.S. Healthcare	45%	61%	76%	83%
Gulf South Health Plans, Inc.	62%	63%	79%	81%
HMO Louisiana, Inc.	Data not available	Data not available	Data not available	Data not available
Maxicare Health Plans, Inc.	Data not available	Data not available	Data not available	Data not available
Ochsner Health Plan	67%	66%	81%	85%
People's Health Network	Data not available	Data not available	Data not available	Data not available
SMA Health Plan, Inc.	59%	69%	81%	88%

APPENDIX L

COMMONWEALTH OF PUERTO RICO

1) **Map of Demonstration Area**
2) **Summary of Local FEHBP Options**
3) **Summary of Medicare+Choice Options**

FEHBP Demonstration: Commonwealth of Puerto Rico

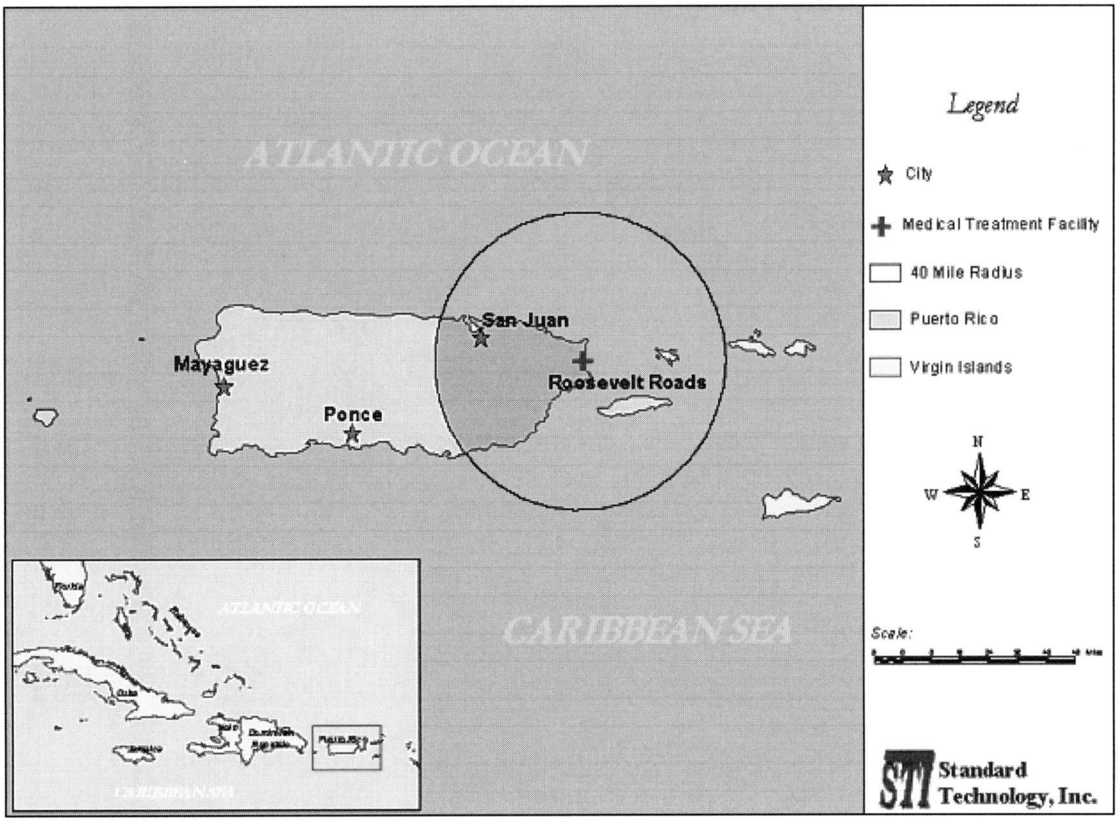

Puerto Rico FEHBP Options

POS									
Triple S – All of Puerto Rico		Primary care doctor	Hospital room copay/ insurance	Prescription drugs, generic	Prescription drugs, brand	Primary care doctor office copay	Hospital inpatient R&B charges	Prescription drugs, generic	R/Brand/ Local
Monthly									
Self only	Self & family								
Your share of premium		In Network You Pay				Out of Network You Pay			
53.50	126.65	$7.50	0	0	$10	$7.50	All over $60/day	0	$10

Puerto Rico FEHBP Quality Indicators

	Satisfaction Indicators 1=above average, 2=average, 3=below average							
Plan Name	Overall plan satisfaction	Getting needed care	Getting care quickly	How well doctors communicate	Courteous and helpful office staff	Customer service	Claims processing	Child survey Overall satisfactoin
Triple S	1	1	3	1	2	1	2	3

Puerto Rico Medicare Supplement Insurance Policies not available

Puerto Rico Medicare Quality Rating data not available